The Curtain is Torn

Receiving Grace from God

Offering Grace in Relationships

Nancy Stark Muyskens

Xulon Press

The Curtain is Torn
by Nancy Stark Muyskens

Printed in the United States of America

ISBN 1-60034-128-4

www.xulonpress.com

Contents

Part I: Death

Part II: Resurrected Life

Acknowledgments

Thanks to all of you who encouraged me to complete *The Curtain is Torn*. There are too many of you to name. This book has been picked up and put down over the course of fifteen years. My friends in Kansas are familiar with an earlier edition of the book. Thank you for your encouragement and your friendship.

Jim and Lois, thank you for your shepherding and your lasting friendship.

Bruce, thank you for the early edit. Sue, thank you for yours as well.

My new friends in Minnesota helped bring this book to the finish line. Thank you Bob, Sandy, Mike S., Connie, Tim, Shelly, Mike O., LuAnn, Mark, and Brenda – my pilot study.

Thank you Paul for your artistic help and computer expertise.

Thanks to all my friends who were more than willing to accept fragmented, incomplete, run-on, or any other kind of sentence. A special thanks to:

My friend Mary Ellen who understands what it is to be desperate. Thanks for your prayers.

My friend Annie who just keeps on loving me.

My friends John and Joyce – We all need rescuing!

My friend Sandy for your tireless efforts at re-editing this book.

Thank you George and Arlene for your Godly heritage. Thank you for accepting me as a Muyskens. I am proud to own your name.

I would also like to acknowledge and give thanks to my parents, Jim and Dorothy, who modeled a graceful, accepting, and forgiving love to their six children. To my "Sibs" – a place where we all get to practice living by our own boundaries and still love each other. Jim B. and Bonnie you are the perfect addition.

Thank you Steve, Sarah, and Emily for being the absolute, tangible, skin on proof that God surely loves me more than I could ever imagine – He gave me you. I love you infinity.

Introduction

"Truly, truly, I say to you, unless a grain of wheat falls into the earth and dies, it remains alone; but if it dies, it bears much fruit. He who loves his life loses it, and he who hates his life in this world will keep it for eternal life" (John 12:24-25).

This book is about death and life, in that order. In our earthly bodies we get confused on that issue. We tend to view things from a life and death perspective. When Christ came, He turned this world and all its thinking upside down. He revealed the true order of things; death leads to life. The natural tendencies that we are born with must die so that a new resurrected life can emerge. To experience freedom in Christ, we must first experience our own personal crucifixion. His crucifixion resulted in resurrection, so will ours. Crucifixion is the avenue by which we can follow Christ into resurrected living.

Jesus' crucifixion made a way for you to have an intimate relationship with God. When Jesus took his last breath on the cross, the great curtain in Solomon's temple that separated the Outer Room (the Holy Place), from the Inner Room (the Most Holy Place), was torn in two by God from top to bottom. The Inner Room is where the presence of God dwelled. Sinful man could not be in the presence of God and live. Jesus took upon Himself all of your sins so that you would qualify to stand in the very presence of God. His life became your perfect sacrifice. The curtain that served to separate man from God is no longer necessary. No more temple with its Inner Room. The curtain is torn; you may stand before God. Stand in His presence, partake of His love, and see what He has planned for you. He plans for you to experience the same victorious life of freedom that Jesus experienced. Jesus has shown us the way to victorious living, and He invites us to follow Him to the cross.

Hallelujah! Freedom is possible. You can talk with God personally in His presence. You can know Him intimately. God has made it possible. He made it possible through the death of His son, Jesus. He led Jesus through crucifixion, and He desires to lead you through it too.

Your crucifixion will not outwardly look like the one Jesus experienced. Yours will look quite unique. It will be solely yours. For many of you, it will come about through the struggles and hurts you experience. Jesus struggled in the garden of Gethsemane prior to His crucifixion. It was there that He was betrayed and abandoned by those who were closest to Him. Like Jesus, much of the hurt done to you will be at the hands of those you love and trust.

Although your crucifixion probably won't involve being nailed to a tree, it will involve the yielding of your will for God's will. Prior to Jesus' crucifixion, He yielded His own will for that of His Father's. "Not my will but thine be done" (Luke 22:42). It is a course that will eventually set you free from the bondage of your will and your way.

Yielding your will to God is not a matter of mustering up enough courage to say to God, "I am yours God, do with me what you will." It is not accomplished through will power and determination. Such *will power* is an exercise of strength. The kind of yielding that leads to crucifixion will happen from a position of weakness, not from one of strength. True yielding takes on the form of abandonment when you find yourself in a position where there is nothing left to say, except, "I am yours God, do with me what you will." You will make the statement to God not from your strength but from your lack of strength. Determination to live the Christian life will be seen as useless. Abandoning yourself to God puts you in a new position of appropriating the Christian life through the power of the Holy Spirit, not determining to live the Christian life in your own strength. True abandonment of your will leaves you in the peaceful, restful position of total reliance on God. You will experience a life that is at last free to receive from God all that He is prepared to give. It is a life of grace. It is a life rich with the blessings that come from being able to see and think clearly with the eyes and mind of God. You will be free to go through life with the ability to make healthy, helpful choices. You will become able to make choices and decisions that will free you and the people you love to live the abundant life that God desires for you to live.

Until this initial crucifixion takes place in your life you will remain vulnerable to all that hinders you from freedom. Your natural self will be bruised and battered over and over again. All of life's struggles and burdens will weigh you down. Injustice will follow you everywhere. You will remain victim not victor. Crucifixion leads to victory. Death leads to victory. Jesus came out of death into resurrected life. There is no victim in Jesus. When Jesus returned from His grave He did not ever make reference to the injustices done to Him. There was no mention of the horrible crucifixion He endured. There was nothing to work through or get over. Bitterness and resentment are never a part of resurrected living.

Crucified:

Crucifixion does not sound inviting does it? And yet, it is the way to life.

~~~~~~~~~~~~~~~~~~~~

> "Then Jesus told his disciples, 'If any man would come after me, let him deny himself and take up his cross and follow me. For whoever would save his life will lose it, and whoever loses his life for my sake will find it'" (Matthew 16:24-25).

~~~~~~~~~~~~~~~~~~~~

You may pick up your cross and follow Jesus to your own crucifixion. It is your call to freedom. Those of you who are resisting crucifixion would perhaps prefer that justice be done. You are waiting for God to reveal to others the injustices done to you. You are at a place where it is quite impossible for you to see any truth about your own condition because you are blinded by the outrageous behavior of others. Perhaps it is even the outrageous behavior of God that offends you. You have fallen victim. I pray that you will wait no longer. Allow the Spirit of truth to put to death all that is within you that is working against you. It is a death that will give way to life.

We will not know crucifixion without knowing the truth. Part of the mystery of life involves seeing the truth. Jesus is the truth. We may start our journey to the cross by asking God to open our eyes to the truth that He desires for us to see.

Please make this your prayer: "Father, I stand before You. The curtain is torn. Reveal to me the truth that You want me to see — the truth about death, and the truth about life. I ask You to, ever so gently, lead me to the place You want me to be."

Part One

Death

"For whoever would save his life will lose it..."
Matthew 16:25

Chapter One

Through the Eyes of a Sinner

"One of the Pharisees asked him to eat with him, and he went into the Pharisee's house, and took his place at table. And behold, a woman of the city, who was a sinner, when she learned that he was sitting at table in the Pharisee's house, brought an alabaster flask of ointment, and standing behind him at his feet, weeping, she began to wet his feet with her tears, and wiped them with the hair of her head, and kissed his feet, and anointed them with the ointment. Now when the Pharisee who had invited him saw it, he said to himself, 'If this man were a prophet, he would have known who and what sort of woman this is who is touching him, for she is a sinner.' And Jesus answering said to him, 'Simon, I have something to say to you.' And he answered, 'What is it, Teacher?' 'A certain creditor had two debtors; one owed five hundred denarii, and the other fifty. When they could not pay, he forgave them both. Now which of them will love him more?' Simon answered, 'The one, I suppose, to whom he forgave more.' And he said to him, 'You have judged rightly.' Then turning toward the woman he said to Simon, 'Do you see this

> woman? I entered your house, you gave me no water for my feet, but she has wet my feet with her tears and wiped them with her hair. You gave me no kiss, but from the time I came in she has not ceased to kiss my feet. You did not anoint my head with oil, but she has anointed my feet with ointment. Therefore I tell you, her sins, which are many, are forgiven, for she loved much; but he who is forgiven little, loves little.' And he said to her, 'Your sins are forgiven'" (Luke 7:36-48).

~~~~~~~~~~~~~~~~~~~~

He who is forgiven much loves much. He who is forgiven little loves little. Jesus is dealing with two different people here. And yet, there really is no difference between them at all; at least not in how God views them. The difference between these two people is in how they see themselves. One of them sees herself very clearly as being a sinner and being in desperate need of God's forgiving grace. The other does not see his sin as clearly, and barely sees himself in need of God's grace.

The Good Life:

Picture in your mind this imaginary person: Jeff was raised in a Christian home. He was involved in a church youth group as a teen, had been on two mission trips before the age of twenty, knows the Ten Commandments and remains accountable to them. He holds others accountable to them also. Jeff lives a clean life. He doesn't smoke, he doesn't chew and he doesn't go with girls that do... Okay, you get the picture.

Now let's try out this scenario: Laura has been married to one man for thirty-five years. She has been faithful to him for all these years. Laura helped raise two kids; both of them have grown to be good Christian citizens. Laura has never stolen, she doesn't lie, and she and her husband have given a tenth of their money every year to the church. She has served in the church faithfully for many years.
~~~~~~~~~~~~~~~~~~~~

They are both beautiful scenarios. A scenario I would be blessed to call my own. My fear, however, for Laura, Jeff, and myself is that because of the comfort and clean living that represents our lives, we may be susceptible to thinking more like the Pharisee in our story and less like the sinner.

How might I respond if I were entertaining an important religious leader and a woman came in weeping and carrying on? What if she started kissing my guest's feet, and then started wiping his feet with her tears and hair? Would I hurry to change the scene? Perhaps try to console her if only to bring about more appropriate behavior? Would I be the one in the story who is cowering off to the side thinking about how unseemly this whole thing looks — feeling a bit uncomfortable? Might I be looking and feeling like the Pharisee in our story? Or would I be found weeping at the feet of Jesus?

Jeff, Laura, you and I have all been forgiven by Jesus. Are we aware, however, of how much we have been forgiven? He who is forgiven much loves much; he who is forgiven little loves little. The problem for each one of us is not that there isn't much to forgive. It is that perhaps we don't see clearly just how very much there is to forgive. Blindness to sin eliminates our perceived need for forgiveness.

Let me tell you another story about a man named David. This story comes out of the Bible also, but I am going to quickly paraphrase it for you. David was a king; a wealthy king. Kings can do pretty much what they want to because they're king. David woke up one morning, looked out of his window and there she was, Bathsheba, the wife of Uriah. One look led to another and before you know it she is pregnant with King David's child. Now Uriah becomes an issue. David wanted to cover up his mistake, so David had Uriah put to death by putting him on the front line in battle where he was sure to be killed.

It is an ugly story. But, that's not the worst of it. It's awful that David committed adultery and tried to cover his sin, and finally had Uriah put to death. But the very worst part of this whole situation is that for nearly a year David remained unrepentant. He did not confess his sin. Why? Because he did not *see* his sin. After all, David was king and kings can pretty much do whatever they want.

The fact that David tried to cover up his mistake indicates that he knew he had a problem. But his response does not demonstrate the remorse and repentance that accompanies the clear understanding of having sinned against God. David's reaction portrays a man who is dealing with a problem, not with sin. Problems are things we simply want to cover up and push aside. It was not until after the birth of their child that God finally sent a prophet, Nathan, to David. Nathan went to David and told him about a rich man who robbed a poor man of his only pet lamb. "Then David's anger was greatly kindled against the man; and he said to Nathan, 'As the Lord lives, the man who has done this deserves to die; and he shall restore the lamb fourfold, because he did this thing, and because he had no pity'" (II Samuel 12:5-6). Nathan looked at David and said, "You are the man." David's eyes were opened and he saw his sin.

On hearing this story, think for a moment of who David was.

- He was the man after God's own heart. II Samuel 23:1 describes him as the "Man who was raised on high, the anointed of the God of Jacob, the sweet psalmist of Israel."
- He had loved and served God from his childhood.
- God had performed countless wonders through him and for him.
- David had praised God more gloriously than any other man.

David was a Godly man. And yet look what becomes of David when God gives him over to the inclination of his own heart for even a moment. Look at how quickly and how deeply he has fallen into sin, and how long he remains unaware of it.

I cannot help but ask myself, if it is that easy for this man who loves God so much *not to see* this sin that we would consider to be so great, then how easy would it be for you or me to not see those sins which we might not consider to be so great? How often do we, like David, consider our transgressions to be problems and not sin? I believe that we often have very little understanding of the magnitude of our sin. We do not see our sin clearly enough. I also believe with all of my heart that we will only experience the incredible grace of God in proportion to how clearly we see our sin.

The very first thing we must realize is that because of our spiritual blindness, we cannot know our sin unless the Spirit of God teaches us to know our sin. We must ask God to do this for us. To ask God, "Teach me to know my sin" is a frightening thought. We don't want to see our sin. I believe that is why there are so few Christians that are experiencing the life that God has intended for us to live. His intention is that we live a resurrected life of freedom. That is His desire for us. Resurrected living can only come by way of crucifixion. Crucifixion only comes by way of the truth. "The truth will set you free" (John 8:32 NIV).

If you want to see your sin the way God wants you to see your sin, ask Him and He will begin to open your eyes to it. God will reveal to you the truth about yourself. When you look to God for teaching and understanding, and ask Him to do it, He will do it, for it is His will that it be done. You will barely feel the need for God's grace until He reveals this truth to you. When God gives you even the smallest glimpse of what you are truly made of, then you are on your way to experiencing a new dimension of God's grace. God wants you to "know the love of Christ which surpasses knowledge, that you may be filled with all the fullness of God" (Ephesians 3:19). The love of Christ will become increasingly clear as you learn to see yourself in truth as you really are. Let this be your prayer: "Father, teach me to know my sin."

God of Wrath – God of Love:

To see oneself as a sinner is not a popular message in today's world. It seems that our society is full of people who are suffering from low self-esteem and lack of self-worth. They do not need religion to throw more negative stuff at them. In order to protect those who need so desperately to be built up and encouraged as being worthy and loved, we have concentrated more on the loving, caring, compassionate side of God, and do not spend much energy looking at Him as the God of wrath and judgment.

Not all that long ago, fire and brimstone was the rage. Preachers would stand up and point their finger at you and do a good job of reminding you of what a wretched sinner you were. It was a message heavy on judgment, light on love. It left people with an incomplete concept of God; not the kind of God you would be quick to run to or want to spend a lot of time getting to know better. They did not find a lot of grace or experience a lot of love. They did not come to know "the fullness of God."

Today, for many people, the pendulum has swung. God is a good guy. He loves you. He gave up His only Son to die for you so that you could have eternal life. It is a very welcome message to an unloved world. It is indeed good news. This new perspective of God has done a good job of bringing people into the flock. Many of us start off with a firm grasp of the welcome news that we are loved, that He gives us eternal life, and that heaven awaits us. Sadly, for many Christians the excitement of this new realization diminishes with time. The good news becomes just that, *good.* Not great, but good. We thank God, and we are really glad for what He did for us, but still the unrest continues. We cease to experience His ongoing grace. We cease to recognize the saving love of God. Not many of us as Christians are truly on our way to knowing "the fullness of God."

I am of the opinion that for any of us to even begin to know "the fullness of God" we must have a very real understanding of both ends of the spectrum, both sides of the pendulum. Judgment and love go hand in hand. To know the love of God, we must look fully into both. To look at one without the other will strip the one of its power. As we begin to understand them both we will begin to experience new dimensions of God's love. We will begin to know love as we have never known it before. Therefore, at the risk of doing something that is not very popular in today's world, I invite you to look at love with me through the eyes of a sinner.

Study Questions

Chapter One
Through the Eyes of a Sinner

In Luke 7:36-48 we learn that "He who is forgiven much loves much." Do you view yourself as one who has *been forgiven much*, one who has *forgiven much*, or simply as one who has *given much*?

____

____

The two people Jesus is dealing with had different perspectives of themselves. What might those perspectives have been?
The Pharisee ______________________________________
The woman who was a sinner __________________________

What do you feel might be God's perspective of each of these two people?
The Pharisee ______________________________________
The woman who was a sinner __________________________

How does our blindness to sin affect our relationship with Jesus?

____

____

Prior to King David's affair with Bathsheba, he was as close to God as any man. Yet even King David finds himself caught in adultery and murder. When we begin to feel least susceptible to the snares of sin is often when we begin to become most vulnerable to sin. What truths might we lose sight of that could make us vulnerable to believing and even participating in lies? ____________________

____

____

How is it that seeing ourselves in truth as we really are can lead us "to a greater understanding and experience of God's grace?

____

____

Do you view God as being more a God of Love, or a God of Judgment? ____________________

What misconceptions can come from viewing Him primarily as a God of Love? ______________________________

____

What misconceptions can come from viewing Him primarily as a God of Judgment? ______________________________

____

Is the "good news" of your salvation as glorious to you today as it was perhaps a few years ago, or has it lost some of its luster?

____

Is a life of ongoing grace a reality to you? ____________________
Do you desire to know "the fullness of God" in an ongoing way?

____

God's grace is always in the forefront when it is looked at through the eyes of a sinner.

Prayer: Lord, teach me to know my sin. I desire to know You in truth. I realize that I must, therefore, see myself in truth. Amen.

Chapter Two

Guilty

"Whoever does not always obey everything that is written in the book of the law is under God's curse!" (Galatians 3:10 GNB)

"For all have sinned and fallen short of the glory of God" (Romans 3:23 NIV).

"There is none that doeth good - no not one" (Romans 3:10 TLB).

I suffered in an abusive marriage relationship. I was a Christian going into the marriage, and believed that I had no other option but to learn to live within it. And so I did, for over five years. Only one couple knew of the nightmare in which I lived, John and Joyce. The reason they did is because on occasion my doctor would request that I not go back home for a while. John and Joyce's home became a place of refuge where I could spend a day to regain my health and strength.

My health finally deteriorated to the point where John, being the good friend he was, could no longer watch. He came to my house one afternoon, went to the closet, pulled out a suitcase, opened it up, threw in a pair of blue jeans, a t-shirt, three pair of underwear, two pair of socks, a toothbrush, and slammed it shut. He threw the suitcase in the car, put me in the car, and said, "You're never coming back here again." I never did.

When John had at long last removed me out from under this bad relationship, I left in very poor health, with no money, no job, no home, and absolutely no self worth. I was destitute. It left me emotionally crippled. I needed help, I knew I needed help, and so I sought help. A professional counselor told me that I would never be able to fit back into the mainstream of life. I had no trouble believing that. I came out of this relationship the victim.

You might think such victims would be the most receptive to God's love. And yet, I fear that they are not. In such an instance, the victim, by comparison, didn't really do anything wrong. The victim is the "good guy." The world was very quick to confirm that belief. Society was quick to pardon me and blame him. He was clearly the one that was in the wrong. Had I received what the world was offering me, it would have been very easy for me to come out of the whole thing as being in the *right.* He was bad and I was good and that's the end of it. But my spirit was not comfortable with that. The Holy Spirit within me was not comfortable, and I am so grateful that He was not, because God's love is not found in that kind of thinking, nor is there any healing in that kind of thinking. I struggled with this for a long time, until, finally, in all my uneasiness, I was able to ask God: "What is it You are trying to tell me? What spiritual truth am I not grasping?" God, in all of His love, was able to tell me, "Nancy, you stand guilty before Me, and you are in need of My grace."

There are many people who, as a result of being a victim, walk away very wounded. We have all been the victim of someone else's sinfulness. It is easy to walk away with a very low self-esteem; with a sense of being defective and inadequate as a human being. We become ingrained with a deep sense of disgrace and shame. We walk away feeling that we are not lovable, acceptable, capable, valuable, or worthwhile. We develop a strong sense that we are very much alone, not belonging anywhere, to anything, or to anyone.[1] It is hard to think that a loving God would add to that heap by calling that wounded person a sinner. But He did just that. God called me a sinner, and He did not stop there. God went on to do something for me that changed my life. He gave me a glimpse into my own heart. God opened my eyes. I saw the truth that was in me. "Thou desirest truth in the inward being" (Psalm 51: 6). I saw the seeds of every sin within my heart. I realized that God alone could keep those seeds from growing. When I saw what was in me there was nothing left for me to do except to take what little there was left of me and get rid of it. There was nothing there worth keeping. Nothing. I learned what I was made out of. I learned that I was made out of sin. In seeing the truth about myself I was ready to allow God to put it to death. What I saw needed to die.

"Behold, I was brought forth in iniquity, and in sin did my mother conceive me" (Psalm 51:5). This verse does not mean that the act of conception is sinful. It means that sin is conceived into me. It is genetic. I am made out of flesh and bone and sin.

I saw what I was made out of, and I realized that sin is not something to be measured. "The soul that sins shall die" (Ezekiel 18:4). We are not less guilty because our sins are less large. We are made out of sin. No longer did I stand wounded before God; I stood guilty before God. As a result, I could no longer hold on to the bitterness, the anger, or the resentment I had toward any person who had "done me wrong," because it was enough for me to worry about my own standing with God. God knew that in order for me to be set free from the sins of others I first needed to see my own sin.

Immediately after God revealed to me what I was made out of, He then revealed to me the perfect solution to my dilemma. It is the perfect solution for all who find themselves standing utterly broken and helpless before God. I realized I was helpless to do anything about my sin. I could only stand before God in truth, admitting that sin is mine. I own it. I cannot remove it and no person on earth can take it from me. God alone can provide escape from the nature into which I was born. But God says to us, "Look at the gift I have for you. It is the gift of My son, Jesus, and His cleansing blood." If you will receive this gift, all of your sin will be taken from you, and you will be filled instead with the very Spirit of God. In receiving this gift you are made as white as snow; you are made entirely clean. To a person who has been defiled, used and abused, this message is the greatest gift there could ever be. In receiving His gift, I was made a brand new creature, with a brand new start.

God set me free from the bondage of sin. Free from my own sin and from the effects of other's sinfulness. In revealing to me my sinfulness, I was free to receive His forgiveness and His life-changing provision for my dilemma — His life for mine. It was the easiest exchange I ever made, once I saw my great need for it.

He who is forgiven little loves little. He who is forgiven much loves much. I was forgiven much! At last I could know the freedom that comes in being able to forgive others.

Free to Forgive:

Many of us have been taught as Christians that we are to forgive. We have been told that forgiveness is a choice. As a result, we will try to muster up enough strength to say to God, "Oh, all right, I forgive." We may even try to sound earnest when we say it. We say it in hopes that those words will take away the enormous pain that goes along with unforgiveness. We learn quickly that words are not enough to rid us of the ugly truth that remains in our heart. The ugly self-destructive thoughts of unworthiness, and/or the ugly residue of hatred are often the truth of what remains after we have offered to God our *choice* to forgive.

Forgiveness is not something we can generate within ourselves. Our natural selves are not made out of the stuff that forgiveness requires. We are naturally made out of "self stuff," not "God stuff." Our focus will turn inward, not upward. This kind of inward thinking leads us farther away from forgiveness. These thoughts lead to bitterness, resentment, hopelessness, unlovability, and unforgiveness.

I am convinced that forgiveness is something that we are incapable of arriving at apart from God intervening in our lives. Forgiveness is not a choice — forgiveness is a miracle. We cannot create miracles; we can only experience them. God desires that we experience freedom from the power of unforgiveness. Thankfully, God is waiting to intervene by providing a way that we can experience the miracle of forgiveness.

"The truth will set you free" (John 8:32 NIV).

When God revealed the truth to me about my own condition, I was set free from the false beliefs that had left me devastated. It was my false beliefs that trapped me with the mindset of the victim. Seeing yourself in truth as you really are will enable you to stretch out your arms on the cross and say, "Put it to death." The freedom that comes with this necessary seeing of the truth is astounding. You will be the victim no more. It will no longer be about what others have done *to* you. It will be about what God has done *for* you.

One of the miracles that goes along with being fully acquainted with your own sin is that you no longer worry about the sins of others. Have you had to forgive someone you loved or trusted? I mean really forgive, the way God does. Have you found yourself unable to do it? Have you found yourself going back to God with the same issue over and over again? Perhaps you have gone through the motions of forgiveness, offering up lip service of forgiveness, but not experiencing it in your heart. Is the bitterness still there, or have you experienced the miracle of forgiveness? When the Spirit of God has made you aware of your own sin, then it will become impossible for you to worry about the sins of others. Then you will indeed experience forgiveness. The conviction of the Holy Spirit leads to freedom, freedom from self-centered living, freedom to forgive, freedom to serve.

Study Questions

Chapter Two
Guilty!

Tell about a time when you were wounded by someone else's sinfulness. ____

____

Tell about a time when someone was wounded because of your sinfulness. ____

____

Some of you will have no trouble thinking of examples to these questions. For you the sinful examples may be large and painful. Others may struggle in answering these questions, thinking that your examples are small and hardly worth mentioning. We often look for the *big sins* when trying to answer questions like these. And yet it is often the ongoing assault of what we might call *little sins* that impact our lives the most. These can have hurtful effects that are all too easily swept under the rug.

Which would most describe you in relation to sin?

____ It is easy for me to dwell on the sins of others and how that affects me.

____ I spend a lot of energy worrying about my own sins and inadequacies.

____ I try not to think about sin at all.

____ I feel free from the weight of sin. (Both my own sin and the effects of other's sinfulness.)

Satan desires to blind us to the truth. He does that by getting us to focus on anything that will steer us away from the truth. When we focus on our woundedness it is usually because we are focusing on someone else's shortcomings (or sins) and how that affects us.

How grateful I am that Jesus is able to look beyond how we wound Him. He loves us regardless of our sinful condition. He is prepared to forgive and renew us even if we should choose not to accept His forgiveness and renewal. His love is freely given; it is not earned or deserved. That is the truth about love.

List some things that can cause you to easily lose sight of the truth about love. (i.e. insensitive spouse, ungrateful children, thankless job, disrespectful coworkers): ______________________________

____

Give some examples of how the people Jesus loved wounded him or let him down: ____

____

____

Did this change His love for them in any way? ______________
Did it deter Jesus in any way from His ultimate mission of love?

____

Prayer: Lord, teach me the truth about Your love. Teach me to know my sin so that I will understand what it is you have forgiven. Enable me, then, to love others in truth (in all of their sinfulness) as You have loved me in truth. Amen.

Chapter Three

The Truth Shall Set You Free

God made me a brand new creature and gave me a brand new start. I experienced freedom from the bondage of sin. King David's prayer became my reality... "Restore unto me the joy of thy salvation, and uphold me with thy free spirit" (Psalm 51:12 KJV).

Freedom in Christ:

~ When we think of freedom in Christ we might think of growing in knowledge to the point where we obtain it. We may think that we have not learned all we need to learn in order to be free.

~ We may try to obtain freedom by climbing the mountain of faith, thinking that when we reach that pinnacle, freedom will be waiting for us. Many are waiting for that "mountain top" experience to provide their long awaited freedom.

~ Or, we may view spiritual freedom in terms of our ability to love others. We might put more effort into being a better person; attempt to love more, give more, and sacrifice more, all in hopes of becoming more holy and thus more free.

~~~~~~~~~~~~~~~~~~~~

I did not come to freedom by growing in knowledge, or by trying to learn to love others better. Freedom did not come to me in any
~~~~~~~~~~~~~~~~~~~~

way through my own efforts, or by improving my Christian walk. Freedom did not come to me on the mountain; it came to me in the valley. When we can be free in the valley, then we are free indeed.

It is important to understand that it was not my circumstances in the valley that led me to freedom. It was truth that led me to freedom. It was God revealing to me the truth about myself that led me to freedom. Circumstances will not lead you to freedom any more than increased knowledge will lead you to freedom. We will all experience great joy and great sorrow in our lifetime. We will not all experience freedom as a result of those joys and sorrows, because circumstances do not lead to freedom. Truth leads to freedom.

David wrote the 51st Psalm after having been in the valley. Did David find freedom as a result of his circumstances? No. He remained unrepentant for nearly a year. His circumstances did not change his heart at all. It was not until God opened his eyes to his sin that he was ushered into freedom through the forgiveness of those sins. Why do I mention this? I have known people to worry and fret over the idea that they would have to experience some awful traumatic experience or be party to some huge sin in order to be broken. We tend to measure sin as being a big sin or a little sin. I call it the Richter scale of sin. There are many who fear that the only way they can grow in faith and in love of God is to experience great loss or heartache. That is the furthest thing from the truth. Freedom is not the result of horrible circumstances; it is the result of the truth. "The truth will set you free" (John 8:32, NIV). There is enough in your heart right now that God can point to in order to reveal His life changing truth.

~~~~~~~~~~~~~~~~~~~~

> "Behold, thou desirest truth in the inward being; therefore teach me wisdom in my secret heart" (Psalm 51:6).

~~~~~~~~~~~~~~~~~~~~

Let's look at Peter's life. We know that Peter loved the Lord. He loved Him so much that he said at the last supper, "Lord, I am ready to go with you to prison and to death" (Luke 22:33). There is no doubt in my mind that he meant it. He loved Jesus. Before the cock crowed that very morning, however, he had denied knowing Jesus three times.

~~~~~~~~~~~~~~~~~~~~

> Then they seized him [Jesus] and led him away, bringing him into the high priest's house. Peter followed at a distance; and when they had kindled a fire in the middle of the courtyard and sat down together, Peter sat among them. Then a maid, seeing him as he sat in the light and gazing at him, said, "This man also was with him." But he denied it, saying, "Woman, I do not know him." And a little later some one else saw him and said, "You also are one of them." But Peter said, "Man, I am not." And after an interval of about an hour still another insisted, saying, "Certainly this man also was with him; for he is a Galilean." But Peter said, "Man, I do not know what you are saying." And immediately, while he was still speaking, the cock crowed. And the Lord turned and looked at Peter. And Peter remembered the word of the Lord, how he had said to him, "Before the cock crows today, you will deny me three times." And he went out and wept bitterly" (Luke 22:54-62).

~~~~~~~~~~~~~~~~~~~~

"The Lord turned and looked at Peter." Truth stared Peter in the face that morning. "Peter remembered the word of the Lord and he went out and wept bitterly." Peter's last memory of Jesus before He died on the cross was of Jesus looking at him in truth as he really was. Peter saw himself as a sinner on that Friday morning, because truth had finally stared him in the face. With that look, all of the wonderful external stuff that represented Peter's ministry for three years (the preaching, healing, and teaching), it all became as filthy rags. Peter's ministry had been too much about himself and his goodness, not about God and His love. Peter had not yet been set free from the bondage of himself and his sin. He had not come to see the truth yet. The truth was not about him being strong and capable, it was about his weakness and inability to live the life that he desired to live. Freedom comes in seeing the truth about our dilemma and appropriating God's solution to the problem. Does that mean we cannot do anything for Jesus before we know freedom? No, you can work yourself to the bone for Jesus and not know freedom.

The Lie of Shame vs. The Truth of Conviction:

When the Holy Spirit *convicts* you of sin, it stems from truth, which leads to freedom. Conviction is a good thing, a necessary thing. However, when the world, the flesh, or the devil *accuses* you of sin, it does not stem from the truth because only Jesus is the truth. Only Jesus can convict and lead us to freedom. When the world, the flesh, or the devil points out your sin, or accuses you of sin, it does not lead to freedom, it leads to bondage, the bondage of shame.

"Shame, shame, shame. Shame on you!" These are words most of us have heard in our lifetime. I despise shame. Jesus does too. In Hebrews 12:2, we read about Jesus, "who for the joy that was set before him endured the cross, despising the shame." Jesus hates sin and despises shame. In despising the shame, Jesus was able to set it aside and not succumb to the effects of shame. We, on the other hand, fail to despise shame and instead we embrace it. We succumb to the effects of shame. Rather than experience freedom by setting aside the shame, we experience bondage by living in shame. The voice of shame offers bondage, so if you are feeling shame, it isn't God talking. Shame is a lie, because it comes from the father of lies. Shame will point its finger at you and say...

- You are no good.
- You fell short again, you are a failure, you never do anything right.
- You're a bad person.
- You are weak.

That is how shame will speak to you. Conviction on the other hand, is truth because it comes from Jesus who is the truth. Now look at how truth deals with the power of lies:

- When the father of lies says, "you're no good," truth says... "Yeah." "For I know that nothing good dwells within me" (Romans 7:18). "There is none that doeth good, no not one" (Romans 3:12 KJV).
- When the father of lies says, "You fell short again, you're a failure, you never do anything right," truth says, "For there is no distinction since all have sinned and fall short of the glory of God" (Romans 3:22b-23). "Not that we are competent of ourselves to claim anything as coming from us, our competence is from God, who has made us competent to be ministers of a new covenant" (II Corinthians 3:5-6).
- When the father of lies points its finger at one ugly deed you have done, truth comes back with, "That's nothing, I am guilty of far more than that."
- When the father of lies says, "You are weak," truth says, "Hallelujah, I am right where God wants me. God's strength is perfected in my weakness. When I am weak then I am strong."

The lying accusations of shame are annihilated by the Spirit's conviction of truth. Shame becomes powerless because it is exposed as a lie and replaced with the truth. Ironically, the truth and the lie look an awful lot alike. The reason they look so much alike is because Satan takes the truth, wraps it up in shame and serves it up to us as a lie. We bite into the lie because it looks so much like the truth.

The lie is:	The truth is:
I am no good.	In me dwells no good thing.
I fell short again.	All have fallen short.
I am weak.	That is where God wants me. When I am weak, then I am strong.

I am worthless.	I am worth the life of God's only son, Jesus Christ.

When Peter went weeping from the outer court after having denied Jesus three times, what thoughts do you suppose were going on in his mind that morning? My guess is he was thinking, "I'm a failure, I'm no good, I'm weak." He was filled with shame. Jesus despises shame and its crippling effects. He wanted Peter to see the truth. What is the truth?

- All have fallen short. "You failed, Peter."
- In me dwells no good thing. "You are a sinner, Peter."
- I am weak. "When you finally come to see your weakness Peter, then you will desire to appropriate my strength."

God wants to reveal truth to you so that you can stop living according to the lies in shame and start living according to the truth in freedom. Like Jesus, we can despise the shame, set it aside, and pick up the conviction of truth.

Peter saw the truth about himself and was now in a position to be loved by Christ. He could not fully receive the love of Christ until he understood the unconditional nature of that love. Peter was ready to tap into the only source of true love.

~~~~~~~~~~~~~~~~~~~~

This scene with Peter could have gone differently than it did. If I had been with Peter, I can just hear myself: "Peter don't be so hard on yourself, after all, you followed Jesus farther than the other disciples. Everyone else, except John, turned tail and ran from the garden. They didn't follow Jesus as far as you did." Peter could have rationalized his behavior away, and convinced himself that he loved Jesus more than most of the others. He could have talked of how his motives were good. Too often we rationalize or excuse our sin by focusing on our good motives. In so doing, we sabotage the work of the Holy Spirit. The Holy Spirit is hard at work trying to convict us
~~~~~~~~~~~~~~~~~~~~

of our sinful nature, and mankind is hard at work reminding us that we are only human.

Jill Briscoe once gave this illustration: "In pro basketball, I can always tell the rookies from the pros because the rookies raise their hand when they foul. They raise their hand. They acknowledge their transgression, so to speak. But, unfortunately, after a few games or seasons, they stop raising their hand. They cease to view it as a transgression, and they begin to view it as being part of the game." [2] How many of us as Christians view sin as being part of the game? Not only might we have the tendency to view sin as being part of the game, we may also have the unfortunate tendency of measuring sin. Is it a big sin or little sin? (As if somehow the little sins are not as bad.) Do we sometimes lie, or are those only "white" lies?

What if we were to put Peter's sin on the Richter scale of sin? Peter denied knowing Jesus. Have any of you ever denied knowing Jesus? Maybe like Peter you just weren't in a friendly crowd. If you have denied knowing Jesus, did it wound you to the very core of your being or was it so low on the Richter scale of sin that it just seemed like part of the game?

Peter's words of denial wounded him to the core of his being. No one was there to sabotage the work of God. Peter stood alone that morning and saw himself differently than he had before. His eyes were opened. He stood *guilty* before God. In that realization he came to know God's love differently than he had known it before. He realized it was not a matter of how much he loved Jesus; it was a matter of how much Jesus loved him. Jesus knew Peter couldn't do it. He had told him the night before at the last supper that Peter would deny Him three times. Jesus was not surprised that morning. The message from Jesus is: "That's why I came. I knew you couldn't do it. I came to do it for you. I came to live the life that I knew you couldn't live. I am going to the cross for you, because you can't do it and I love you." The love of God is such that it is not based upon our faithfulness to God but upon His faithfulness to us. The beauty of seeing ourselves as we really are is that it helps us to see God as He really is. He is a God who loves us first and loves us last. He is prepared to pour out on you His immeasurable grace.

In the previous chapter, I challenged you to ask God to teach you to know your sin. It is a radical concept, considering we often work so hard to cover up our sin in order to look good in our own eyes and in the eyes of other people. Self-deception is one of our most fine-tuned coping mechanisms. Truth, however, is essential to freedom. The truth is what will set you free.

Study Questions

Chapter Three
The Truth Shall Set You Free

Have you ever felt as though freedom in Christ was something that people talked about but was not really obtainable? The Bible tells us that we can be set free. It also tells us what will set us free. "The ____________will set you free" (John 8:32 NIV).
We know that freedom will not come by any other avenue than Jesus Christ. Jesus claims that He is the truth. "I am the way, the truth, and the life" (John 14:6). Therefore, it is Jesus who reveals truth to us.

The truth is often difficult to hear. That is why we as Christians are often too quick to rescue people from having to come face to face with the truth. Can you think of some ways in which we may inadvertently sabotage the work of the Holy Spirit in our own life or the lives of others? ____

____

____

____

It is very important, however, that we realize it is not our job to convict people of sin. Only the Holy Spirit can do that. It is not my job to go to you with a list of things I believe God is trying to teach you. It is only for me to gently and quietly respond to you as I am in relationship with you. As brothers and sisters in Christ, we can help to affirm truth for each other. Satan likes to take a lie and make it look like the truth. When we believe that distortion of the truth, it leaves a crippling residue of bondage and shame.
Why is it so easy for us to not recognize a lie when it is put before us? What does Satan like to do to confuse us? ____________________

____

____

When the Holy Spirit convicts you of sin it stems from truth, which leads to ______________. When the world, the flesh or the devil accuses you of sin it does not come from truth (Jesus); it leads to ____________________.

Jill Briscoe gave an illustration using pro-basketball. It demonstrated how easy it is for us to begin to view sin as being "part of the game." List some of the *infractions* that are so commonplace in our society today that they would simply be viewed as being part of the game. ____

____

____

____

God is faithful to us even when we are not faithful to him. God loved us first and He loves us always. Do not be afraid to go to God in truth as you really are. He desires to meet you in truth. Give Him all that is in your heart. Give Him all your burdens, failures, hopes, fears, joys and dreams. Today I will only start you in prayer...

Prayer: Lord, I meet You today in truth as I really am. I invite You to look into my innermost heart and see all that is there. I ask You to shed light on what You see so that I, too, may see it. I cannot give you what is in my heart if I do not see it. These are the things I see…

Chapter Four

The Curtain is Torn

Why do you suppose Jesus waited until He did to reveal the truth to Peter about his own weakness — the truth about his inability to live up to his professed loyalty to and love for Jesus? Jesus had been working intimately with Peter for three years. Surely He could have done it sooner. Why did He wait to open Peter's eyes? One reason may be because Jesus was preparing, at that very point in history, to make way for the Holy Spirit to play a whole new role in the lives of His people. Provision was being made for Peter so that he could, in just a short while, appropriate the power of the Holy Spirit. A new covenant was made, because at last a new covenant was possible. Would God point out Peter's insufficiency only to leave him insufficient? Never!

Jesus was on His way to the cross when He opened Peter's eyes to his sinfulness. The moment Jesus died on the cross, the curtain in the Temple that separated the Outer Room (The Holy Place) from the Inner Room (The Holy of Holies) was torn in two from top to bottom. At that moment we no longer needed to be kept from God's presence. We could once again stand before God. Provision had been made for our sin through the redeeming blood of Jesus Christ. The presence of God desires to take up residency in a new temple... You. Peter would soon go from a crushing outer courtyard experience to a miraculous Inner Room experience.

~~~~~~~~~~~~~~~~~~~~

> "Nevertheless I tell you the truth: it is to your advantage that I go away, for if I do not go away the counselor will not come to you; but if I go, I will send him to you" (John 16:7).
>
> "Such is the confidence that we have through Christ toward God. Not that we are competent of ourselves to claim anything as coming from us; our competence is from God, who has made us competent to be ministers of a new covenant, not in a written code but in the Spirit; for the written code kills, but the Spirit gives life" (II Corinthians3:4-6).

~~~~~~~~~~~~~~~~~~~~

We are ministers of a new covenant. It is a covenant that can be lived out - but only in the Spirit. Jesus wants Peter to be ready to receive what Jesus Himself is providing through His death.

- Complete forgiveness of sins,
- Made entirely clean,
- Sinless... so that God himself can enter into His new temple. YOU!!

The curtain is torn. You have become the Holy of Holies. The Spirit of God can now make His home in you. The only one who will receive God's provision is the one who sees a need. If Peter had remained blind to his need, he would not have been prepared to receive the fullness of God. The future of the church rested on Peter. Peter was the rock upon which Jesus chose to build His church. It is good that truth stared Peter in the face that Friday morning in the outer courtyard. Peter was ready to exchange his life for Christ's.

God provided the blood of Jesus so that we qualify to spend eternity in heaven with him. Your salvation is secure when you accept Jesus as Savior. But His provision does not end there. His blood saves. His Spirit empowers. He doesn't save us just so we can experience the Christian life in heaven. He saves us so that we can begin to experience the Christian life here on earth today.

<u>Supernatural Living:</u>

When Jesus appeared to the disciples for the first time after His resurrection from the dead, what was the first thing He did? What was His agenda?

~~~~~~~~~~~~~~~~~~~~

> "On the evening of that day, the first day of the week, the doors being shut where the disciples were, for fear of the Jews, Jesus came and stood among them and said to them, "Peace be with you." When he had said this, he showed them his hands and his side. Then the disciples were glad when they saw the Lord. Jesus said to them again, "peace be with you. As the father has sent me, even so I send you. And when he had said this, he breathed on them, and said to them, "Receive the Holy Spirit" (John 20:19-22).

~~~~~~~~~~~~~~~~~~~~

Wow! "Receive the Holy Spirit!" At that point in history it became an option. God tore the curtain from top to bottom. Spirit of God, enter in. We can experience a life of walking in and with the Spirit of God. We can live in the power of God's Holy Spirit. That is God's intention for you and me. God's intention, now that the curtain is torn, is that we experience what J. Packard calls "supernatural living." "We are called out of the natural and into the supernatural. We are not just to be nice products of a secular world. We are new creatures, living supernatural lives. It is a life where folks will see it, but not understand it. It will bewilder them. A life that displays the fruits of the Spirit: a love which makes others great rather than themselves, a joy in all things, peace in all situations, patience where it would otherwise be impossible, and on it goes. For us the supernatural can become natural."[3]

God desires to put an end to our natural way of living, so that we can continue on with the supernatural. Allow the Holy Spirit to do His work in you. First, ask Him to open your eyes to the truth, so that you will gladly give to God what He asks of you - your life. And second, that you can go on to experience the resurrected life in the Spirit.

This supernatural life or this abundant life that Scripture talks about is there to be had for every believer. This life is not something we achieve; it is something we receive. We don't attain it; we obtain it. We cannot earn it; we cannot win it. We can do nothing except ask, receive, and thank the giver. It is a gift of God that we can receive through Jesus because of what He has done for us.

We cannot take credit for any part of God's gift of transformation in our lives. We cannot point to our own wisdom or good deeds. We can only point to a generous God, with an enormous love for us. The supernatural life will become ours as we truly seek after God and all He is prepared to give. Everything about our life in Christ is a gift, from beginning to end. God is the giver, and we are the receivers. The gift does not go to those who do great things. It goes to the one who is willing to receive great things. It is a simple concept and yet it is one that is easily lost sight of.

Too often Christians fail to experience supernatural living because they fail to receive the necessary work of the Holy Spirit. It is not just an indwelling of the Spirit that we need. It is the purifying work of the Spirit as well.

In the next two chapters we will attempt to look at two specific hindrances that can keep us from experiencing the cleansing work that needs to take place in our lives. We will explore two areas that often prevent us from experiencing the crucifixion of the natural tendencies that live within us. It is a process necessary to a life of freedom. These two hindrances are wounds, and works. We will also see how God intends for both of these things not to hinder our progress toward resurrected life, but actually lead us to that life.

Study Questions

Chapter Four
The Curtain is Torn

The curtain is torn! Spirit of God, enter in! Jesus saves with His blood. He empowers with His Spirit. Thus, "[God] made us competent to be ministers of a new covenant, not in a written code but in the Spirit, for the written code kills, but the Spirit gives life" (II Corinthians. 3:6).

What qualifies us to be ministers of this new covenant?

___ The written code
___ Reading the Bible
___ Doing lots for the church
___ The Holy Spirit

Many of us attempt to be ministers of God. Unfortunately, we often attempt it in our own strength, apart from the Spirit. For us to attempt it at all is futile. Jesus is not just a standard that we are to live up to as best we can. He is our Savior, and He has given the Holy Spirit to us in order that we may experience life in the Spirit.

The Holy Spirit is evidenced in our lives by certain fruit. Please list the fruit of the Spirit.

________________ ________________ ________________
________________ ________________ ________________
________________ ________________ ________________

We all know what these qualities look like. Therefore, we all know how to imitate them. I am not talking about a life that imitates the fruit of the Spirit; I am talking about a life that displays the genuine Spirit of God when man would not be able to.

Scripture teaches us how to discern real fruit from imitation fruit.

Imitators of fruit: "If you love those who love you, what credit is that to you? For even sinners love those who love them. And if you do good to those who do good to you, what credit is that to you?

For even sinners do the same. And if you lend to those from whom you hope to receive, what credit is that to you? Even sinners lend to sinners, to receive as much again" (Luke 6:32-34).

It is time to take another hard look at ourselves. How often do our lives resemble this cheap kind of love that belongs to *sinners*? It is easy for me to love those who love me. I'm good at returning their love. I am kind and do good to those who are kind and do good to me. I am really good at that too. And I would be quick to loan to most of my fellow Christians anything they might need, knowing that they would undoubtedly return the favor.

The question that we must ask ourselves is, "Does my life demonstrate what scripture describes as genuine fruit?"

Genuine fruit: "But I say to you that hear, love your enemies, do good to those who hate you, bless those who curse you, pray for those who abuse you. To him who strikes you on the cheek, offer the other also; and from him who takes away your coat do not withhold even your shirt. Give to everyone who begs from you; and of him who takes away your goods do not ask them again. And as you wish that men would do to you, do so to them" (Luke 6:27-31).

Is this the life that describes you? Perhaps this is another opportunity for us to look truthfully at ourselves. It surely is for me. In truth, I often look more like the imitator of fruit, which is not fruit at all. But I know for a fact that we can experience the splendid life of grace and love that displays the genuine fruit of God's Holy Spirit. I have tasted, if even for a moment, the freedom there is in being able to "love your enemies." Let's not settle for the cheap taste of imitation love.

Have you ever imitated the fruit of the Spirit in your own strength? ___________________.

Write about a time when you attempted to do that. ____________

____

____

Have you experienced a time when the Holy Spirit clearly demonstrated the genuine fruit of love in your life? _________________.

Write about a time when you experienced that. ________________

____

____

Because you have been made clean by the blood of Jesus, the Holy Spirit has now entered into you. He did not enter you with only some of the characteristics of God. God cannot be divided. The Holy Spirit enters you with the fullness of God. God in you! Wow!

The list of spiritual fruit that describes the Holy Spirit can now become a list of words that describe you and me. It is possible! We must yield to the Holy Spirit who lives in us. Thanks be to Jesus - the curtain is torn.

Prayer: Spirit of God, have Your way with me.

Chapter Five

Wounds

Emotional wounds can cut deep. They are personal and they can be crippling. Emotional wounds are personal in that it is about *you*. It is about the *self* in you that you are trying so hard to keep alive and well. We want to fix our wounds by building up our *selves* so that we can feel good about our *selves* again. These wounds, given to God, could be used to bring about the necessary crucifixion in our lives, the result being a new, resurrected way of life. Too often, however, Satan takes hold of those hurts and uses them to keep us stuck in a dark and lifeless place. Satan likes the condition of spiritual lifelessness that we are born into. He wants to keep us in that lifeless condition. Wounds are just the thing to do it.

While Jesus walked this earth He met multitudes of tired, wounded people. His advice to all of them was this: "Come to me."

<u>Come to Me:</u>

> "Come to me, all who labor and are heavy laden, and I will give you rest. Take my yoke upon you, and learn from me; for I am gentle and lowly in heart, and you will find rest for your souls. For my yoke is easy, and my burden is light" (Matthew 11:28-30).

Jesus says, "Come to me." Jesus knows there is no other place to find rest. There is no other place to find wholeness, forgiveness, grace, love, or life. Jesus is the source of all this and more. If this is what you are looking for, Jesus says, "Come to me." Don't look for it anywhere else because you will not find it. Rest will only be found at the feet of Jesus.

The fact that we need to go to someone at all indicates that we have a need. When we are not feeling in need of anything we do not need anyone. At those times we are feeling quite self-sufficient. Self-sufficiency keeps us from relying on God. When all is right with the world we tend to spend less time in fellowship with Jesus. One of mankind's greatest weaknesses is our ability to live autonomously. We view self-reliance as a virtue and self-sufficiency as a strength. More often than not, our self-sufficiency keeps us from becoming and remaining completely dependent on God.

During those smooth times in life our first source of help tends to be self, rather than God. We look to ourselves for fulfillment. Physically, emotionally, and even spiritually we try to meet our own needs. We meet those needs through our behaviors and activities. We measure all our self-efforts at wellness by how we are perceived by others. We view ourselves as being "all right" based on how others respond to who we are. If others respond positively to us, we are okay. When others respond negatively to us we run into problems. Our identities can easily be shattered by an unkind remark or an act of unfairness. Woundedness tends to strip us rather quickly of our self-sufficiency and can suddenly make us feel like less of a person. Emotional woundedness is a very real and painful thing especially when it comes from someone we love; someone that we expect to receive love from; someone that we hope to receive good things from and not bad things. It can be devastating when someone we expect to be built up by cuts us down. For some, this is an ongoing experience. For many, it is a way of life. The effects of these emotional wounds eventually strip a person of their ability to rely on themselves as a source of wellness, because there is no wellness in them. The well runs dry. They need another source.

Who Do You Go To?:

Do you rely on yourself or others to fill you up and make you feel good about yourself? Is your identity put in anything other than God?

- Your husband
- Your wife
- Your weight
- Your beauty
- Your job
- Your children
- Your home
- Your title
- Other's opinions of you

Do any of these things determine how you feel about yourself? These forms of idolatry are not easily recognized. Jeff VanVonderen, author of *Tired of Trying to Measure Up*, defines idolatry this way, "Idolatry means basing your sense of life, value, and acceptance on something other than God."[4]

~~~~~~~~~~~~~~~~~~~~

> Mrs. Gunderson keeps her house perfect because she would feel like less of a person if someone were to see her house looking anything less than perfect. Her friends know that about her and agree, "That's just how she is."
>
> Ann Carson frequently lets her husband know that if he really loved her he would make more of an effort to please her. He has resolved to himself, "That's just how she is, so I'd better try harder."
>
> Mary Lou's motivation for going back to work is that she wants to feel like she is a productive,
~~~~~~~~~~~~~~~~~~~~

contributing member of society. She wants to feel important. Her children have resigned themselves to the fact that, "Mom needs to do that for herself."

Marjorie would love to be more involved in the church, but her husband does not have the same desire. Since he is the spiritual head of the home, she must not go on spiritually without him. She'll wait for him to take the lead.

Matt's father is constantly telling him if he would just practice harder he could do better in sports. Matt doesn't really like sports, but he thinks to himself, "That's Dad, He always wants me to be better than I am and be somebody I'm not."

~~~~~~~~~~~~~~~~~~~~

Is your identity based on Jesus and His opinion of you, and on His performance on your behalf? Or is it based on someone else's opinion of you, and the performance of yourself or someone you love? There are many of us who to some degree look to things other than God to determine who we are. It is hard to call that a life of sin. But in order to be free from the bondage of that sin and its harmful effects we need to call it what it is, sinful idolatry. When we seek love and acceptance from some source other than God, we can usually point to an experience in life that has caused us to desire or seek out that acceptance.

~~~~~~~~~~~~~~~~~~~~

Mrs. Gunderson keeps her house clean because her mother taught her that she was not a good wife or mother if it wasn't clean.

Ann Carson heard the same line passed between her parents as a child, "If you really loved me you would perform for me."

Mary Lou learned from her father that her "title" in the world determined her importance in the world.

The church taught Marjorie what it means to be submissive to her husband. She was given a false idea of what it means for her husband to be the head of the home. Her spiritual identity is based on her husband's spiritual identity.

Matt doesn't know who he is yet because he has never been given the chance to explore his own interests.

~~~~~~~~~~~~~~~~~~~~

It is easy to blame others for our low self-esteem and lack of self worth. It is easy because it is often true. We could all point to reasons for why we are the way we are. Someone placed too heavy a burden on our lives. Someone wrongly taught us what makes us valuable and we believed that person. Unfortunately, when all these other sources prove to be insufficient we still do not turn to Jesus. Instead, we will often turn to the very source that inflicted our wounds.

<u>You Wounded Me; You Fix Me!:</u>

In hopes of being loved and accepted by the one we so desperately want to be loved and accepted by, we return to the one who wounded us thinking that they must make things right. We expect that healing can only come from the one who wounded us. We want them to see their wrongdoing and understand the ugly effects of their sinfulness. We get trapped into thinking that not until they feel remorse and beg for forgiveness can we become well. If a certain person or persons caused the problem, then it is only natural that we would go to them in hopes that they will fix it and make it right. That, however, could be a long and futile wait for some of us.

Don't look to people. If people have already proven to be ineffective in meeting your emotional needs, if they are the root of the problem to begin with, then do not go back to the same source in
~~~~~~~~~~~~~~~~~~~~

hopes of finding a cure. Don't throw yourself from the frying pan back into the fire. Find a different source.

Even if you did receive complete remorse from those by whom you were wounded, you would still find yourself in need. If they were to seek you out and beg forgiveness, you would find no cure there — no cure at all. What you would find is that healing does not come in them seeing their need for forgiveness, but in your being able to forgive. Their asking for forgiveness will not make you able to give it. They are not the source from which you will find help. Jesus is the source. Jesus says, "Come to me" and I will show you the way to forgiveness. "Come to me" and experience the love and acceptance that you are so desperately longing to find.

~~~~~~~~~~~~~~~~~~~

Jesus does not desire that we be strengthened in the flesh in order to go back to self-reliance. He desires that our reliance on self would be destroyed. Our life in the flesh must be exposed for what it is, a feeble and powerless attempt at life. Jesus wants to replace our fleshly ways with Spirit filled ways. He desires that we be strengthened not in the flesh, but in the Spirit. If we are built up in the flesh then we remain vulnerable to a life of woundedness and hard work. Therefore, rather than defending ourselves with all the good reasons we have for our false identity, we first need to agree with God. Agree with Him that we sometimes look to sources other than Him for strength and love. These other sources provide nothing more than temporary solutions, and will only restore us to a powerless dependence on self and others.
~~~~~~~~~~~~~~~~~~~

Study Questions

Chapter Five
Wounds

How do you feel when people say kind and wonderful things about you? ____

____

How do you feel when people say hurtful or negative things about you? ____

____

We often rely on ourselves or on others to make us feel good about ourselves. Jeff VanVonderen defines idolatry in this way, "Idolatry means basing your sense of life, value, and acceptance on something other than God."

What is your identity built on? (Ask God to reveal this to you.)

____

____

What is your most recent emotional wound? __________________

____

How did you go about trying to fix your woundedness? Who did you go to? ____

____

What did that person say that made you feel better? ____________

____

____

Do you feel the truth was spoken so that you were brought into a powerful renewal by the Holy Spirit, or were words spoken that simply restored you to the same vulnerable position you were in prior to being wounded? ________________________________

____

What might the Spirit of Truth say to you about this incident that wounded you? (Ask Him.) ____________________________

____

____

God never delights in our hurts or sorrows. On the contrary, He mourns with those who mourn, and weeps with those who weep. God knows how to take the injury that is done to us and turn it into something good. What Satan means to harm us with, God will take and turn into something good. God does not plan the hurtful thing in order to teach you a lesson. He simply takes the inevitable sufferings that will fall upon each one of us as we live in this fallen world, whether it is suffering from someone else's sinfulness, or from a sinful choice of our own, and he uses those sufferings to build within us a character that cannot be shattered. He creates in us the very character and strength that is His own.

Is there a hurt that you may have experienced long ago, that in looking back on you can see how God has managed to take that ugly experience and do something with it that is beautiful? __________

____

____

____

Is there a hurt in your past that you have not yet let go of? Please put that hurt in God's hands, for He desires to take that burden from you. Watch and see what He will do with it. God alone is able to deal with that hurt. We are helpless, in ourselves, to get rid of it. Without the help of God, that hurt can do nothing except grow bigger and dig deeper into your heart. The hurtful effects of wounds are far reaching when left apart from God.

Prayer: Jesus, I fear I am a victim of wounds. The insult to "myself" has been very hurtful, but the greatest harm is that it has prevented me from seeing the truth. Instead of these wounds leading me to You, they have kept me from You. Lord Jesus, I lay these burdens down before You. Thank You that You desire to have them, and that You know what to do with them. I ask that You would cleanse my heart, mind, and body from the ugly effects of these wounds, and that You would recreate me to be all that You intend for me to be. Thank You that Your cleansing leaves me perfectly clean, as white as snow, and totally forgiven. Teach me to put my identity in You, for I am fully loved and accepted by You. Amen.

Chapter Six

Performance Based Living:
An outgrowth of woundedness

I like to be liked. If there is something I can do to ensure that you will like me, I am apt to do it. I don't like criticism. It wounds me. I protect "myself" from being wounded by performing in a way that helps me avoid criticism. My behaviors can, in many cases, prevent me from being emotionally wounded. Therefore, I will watch my behaviors and be very careful about what I say. I will do my best to measure up. I will put your interests above my own, knowing then you will surely like me. In the event that I fail to please you, I will hang my head and remember to try harder next time.

~~~~~~~~~~~~~~~~~~~~

Do you get tired just thinking about the life I have described above? I hope so. God intends for that kind of life to make you tired. So tired, in fact, that you would be willing to give it up.

I Can Do It!:

The fact is, we can control the outcome of a lot that goes on around us. It helps to develop an attitude of, "I can do it!" Too many of us believe that by controlling our lives and our performance we
~~~~~~~~~~~~~~~~~~~~

can help to determine what other people think of us. If we perform well, others will perceive us as being capable, valuable and worthy of being loved. Performing well not only dictates what others think, it also dictates what we think and feel about ourselves. An outstanding performance makes us feel acceptable, lovable, and worthy of other's respect and admiration. This is too often the mindset of many hurting people. With our entire identity at stake it is no wonder we hold on to the arduous lifestyle of performing. Unfortunately, this life of performing is incapable of providing the healthy identity we long for. All of the hard work by which we live will not make us the least bit more valuable, acceptable, or lovable. We are already fully loved, fully accepted, and of infinite value to God.

My daughter has a hamster that spends a good deal of time in an exercise wheel. He runs round, and round, and round, and gets nowhere. In the same way, many people strive to find ways to feel loved and accepted where there is no hope of arriving at such a goal. Acceptance that comes out of performance is conditional, and it will not serve to fill a void that can only be filled by unconditional acceptance and love.

Performance-based living is not only related to the internal making of our identity, it is also closely attached to the external roles we play in society. It involves the demands and expectations that go along with being a mom, dad, wife, husband, employee, employer, student, friend, etc. In today's world the demands of life can be overwhelming. Performance based living requires an unending supply of energy. It is a requirement that our human bodies cannot live up to. We only have a limited supply of energy. Eventually, we run out of energy; we get tired. Today's society calls it "burn out." We work hard, and if that's not good enough, we work harder. It is a life of performing.

In our own strength, this life of performing is a life of doing our best to measure up. It is a life of trying to live up to the expectations that we place on ourselves and that are placed on us by other people. We have expectations being put on us, it seems, in practically every area of our lives; at home, at work, at school, in relationships, in the church. There are a lot of overworked, overtired, stressed out, burned out people in our churches today and in the world today. We are all doing our best to measure up. Sometimes we do and sometimes we don't. We simply go through life performing as best we can for each other. But this life of performing is not the life God has intended for us to live. We are not here to perform or to live up to mankind's expectations of us. That kind of pressure is binding and it causes us to function less and less well, until finally, we are overcome by the expectations that people and the world have placed on us.

God desires that we be free from the weight of all these expectations. He is the one who provides a spirit that is free. Psalm 51 teaches us that we can be upheld by a "free" spirit; God's Holy Spirit; the Spirit that lives in us. We can be free from a life of trying to measure up. Free from oppression, free from fear, free from doubt, and free in relation to mankind. We are not here to perform. God desires that we be free!

While there are many who suffer from wounds, there are equally as many who suffer from the pressures that come with a life of performing — a life of simply trying to meet the demands of the world in which we live. I have found both of these things, wounds and performance based living, to be major cripplers in the lives of people I meet. Jesus has the same response to the burden of all those demands... "Come to me."

<u>I Can't Do It!:</u>

"Come to me".... right now, just as you are. "Come to me... you will find rest." There are no prerequisites for us before we go to Jesus. You do not need to boost your spirits, or muster up enough spiritual strength to do it. You do not need to wait until you get some measure of relief from your weariness. Do not go to Him with any false piety or fancy words. Simply go. In all of your weariness; with all of your failures; with your impoverished spirit; with all of the expectations that the world puts on you, go to Jesus. The world can put a lot of expectations on us. The world burdens us with a list of things that are considered socially acceptable...

- Keeping your house up to a standard.
- Keeping your appearance up to a standard.

- If you have kids, it might be how your kids are expected to behave in school or at grandma and grandpa's house.
- Those same kids probably expect to open their dresser drawer every morning and find clean socks and underwear.
- Your husband comes home at the end of the day and is expecting to find a hot meal on the table.
- Your wife expects you to be home to eat that hot meal while it is still hot.
- Many women work outside the home. You are expected to hold down a job and see that the above list is taken care of.
- You are expected to bring home the bacon, fry it up in a pan, and never let him forget he's a man!
- Men today are expected to be sensitive, compassionate, and masculine.
- And we have not mentioned the expectations that the church puts on you.

Jesus knows about all of these expectations; and He says: "Come to me, all you who are weary"... right now, just as you are... and you will find rest.

There is no such thing as "making yourself ready" to face Jesus. There is nothing you can "do" to make yourself fit for it. "Doing" is an external thing. There is no external expectation in His invitation when He says, "Come to me." The first thing we learn when we go to Jesus is that our problem is not external — it is internal. We have an internal problem. Jesus says, "Learn from me; *for I am gentle and lowly at heart* and you will find rest for your souls" (Matthew 11:29b).

The rest we find in Jesus comes not in doing, but in being — being like Jesus. The rest comes from our learning to be gentle and lowly of heart. It is an internal thing not an external thing. That is exciting news because it means that our rest is not contingent on external things.

How many times in our weariness have we thought, "I need a vacation! I need to get away from this tiring, monotonous grind: the work schedule, the family expectations, the church responsibilities. I need to get away!" And yet we learn from Jesus that our rest is not contingent on any of those things. What a relief that is, because I do not see any of those things going away. They will all be waiting for you when you get back from that vacation. At days end your mom and dad are going to be the same people they were yesterday. Your boss is going to have the same expectations when you walk into work Monday morning. Your teachers and coaches right now are planning what it is they are going to expect from you next week. Your wife, husband, children, friends; they will each have their own set of expectations. The rest we find in Jesus comes not in doing — but in being like Jesus. How then can I be like Jesus? How can I enter into this life of rest? In and of ourselves, there is nothing we can *do* to become like Jesus. There are many ways in which we may try to acquire this life of rest:

- We may brace ourselves in prayer to receive it from God, thinking, "if I just pray harder."
- We may try to copy those who have it.
- We might set up rules by which to live.

These are all good things. But these things alone will not provide ongoing "rest for your souls." It has been proven over and over again that will power does not change people, time does not change people, and sacrifices of service do not change people. In his book *Tired of Trying to Measure Up*, Jeff VanVonderen writes, "We have an internal problem and no amount of positive external behavior is capable of producing an internal transformation."[5] We need to be transformed. Internally we need to be made new. In Part II of this book we will look at the resurrected life and how transformation is possible. We can experience supernatural living by the internal transformation of our minds.

God wants to change your heart and mind. You might think that this is an impossibility, but it is not. The curtain is torn! It is possible, because the Spirit of God lives in you. Right now you are tired of all that life imposes on you. Transformation may sound like yet another task. Not so. It is not your doing; it is God's. Simply invite Him to speak truth to you. You will find God's transforming truth to be like balm to your soul. "Come to me," says Jesus, "and you will find rest for your souls." That rest will come in being like Jesus, not in doing another task. His transforming truth will give you a mindset that cannot be shattered by criticism. His truth will set you free.

Study Questions

Chapter Six

Performance Based Living: An outgrowth of Woundedness

List some of the expectations that you live with daily:

____

____

____

____

____

____

Do you sometimes feel as though your success or failure as a person is determined by how well you live up to these expectations?

____

Many Christians view the sanctification process as simply working hard at self-improvement. We are to try harder to love people, force ourselves to give more, etc. It is easy to get caught in the idea that in order to become like Jesus we are simply to work harder at being good. In attempting to live a good Christian life we "do" lots of good stuff until we finally collapse from fatigue. We think that success as a Christian is demonstrated through our external behaviors. The problem becomes not being able to measure up to all the expectations and external behaviors that the Christian life demands from us.

This chapter teaches us that we do indeed have a problem, but the problem is not external, it is ______________________________

Jeff VanVonderen, author of *Tired of Trying to Measure Up*, writes, "We have an internal problem and no amount of positive external behavior is capable of producing an internal transformation!"

In what ways have you tried to become like Jesus apart from the Holy Spirit's involvement? ____________________

____

____

> "Come to me, all who labor and are heavy laden, and I will give you rest. Take my yoke upon you, and learn from me; for I am gentle and lowly in heart, and you will find rest for your souls. For my yoke is easy, and my burden is light" (Matthew 11:28-30).

Jesus invites us… "Come to me," and "learn from me." What will we learn from Jesus when we go to Him? ____________________

____

Jesus desires that we be free from the yoke of external expectations and that we instead take on His yoke. His yoke is light, because His yoke is not external. We learn from Him gentleness, meekness, humility, and lowliness of heart. These qualities are what will set us free from a life of performing. Free from feeling we need to be the best. Free from striving to be accepted and loved through our behaviors and actions. The humble heart looks not to itself, but to others. Gentleness does not strive; it gives. Lowliness of heart allows us to lift up others and not feel the need to be lifted up ourselves. To be like Jesus is to be free.

What must we "do" before we face Jesus? ____________________
How do we go before Jesus? ____________________

Jesus desires we go to Him in truth, just as we are. If you were to go before Jesus right now, in truth, what would you put before Him? (What things are foremost in your mind: thoughts, feelings, fears, frustrations) ____________________

____

____

Prayer: Jesus, sometimes I fail to spend my time in Your presence because I think that I have to prepare myself somehow to talk to You. I feel as though I need to prepare my heart first by trying to hide the busy, anxious, sometimes hateful thoughts I'm having, and replace those thoughts with calmer, more controlled thoughts. Help me to respond to Your call, "Come to me." Thank You for desiring that I come to You just as I am. How I long to experience the rest You promise in response to that call.

Chapter Seven

Works

As Christians, too many of us fail to experience supernatural living because we fail to find our way to the cross. We see no need for the cross. Crucifixion is not something we desire to receive from God. We would prefer to find another way of obtaining the supernatural life, perhaps through our own efforts. There are many of us who think that having been saved by faith, we are now to live by works and effort. So instead of continuing to receive, we now begin to *do*!

It is an easy trap to fall into, because prior to receiving the gift of salvation through Jesus we lived life in our own strength, in the flesh as the Bible calls it. Going back to living life in our own strength (the flesh) is simply going back to what we already know. And life in the flesh is simply a life of "doing."

The unfortunate truth is that there are many of us who forfeit the abundant life that God intends for us to experience because we cease to receive from God all that He is prepared to give, and we begin to live the Christian life in our own strength. We go back to what we know. Too often, Christians are ushered into this life of performance through the very people group that should be leading them out of it. I refer to the Church.

It breaks my heart when I see Christians attempting to live the Christian life under the custodial care of the "law." I can tell you the outcome of such an attempt. You will fail. And yet, we inflict on each other the burden of upholding the law, when all we have to uphold it with is our will power and determination. We do not usher them into the resurrected life that alone can produce victorious living.

The Church, too often, has nothing more to offer its people, than a tiring, burdensome list of "do's and don'ts" that they must do their best to live by. This is not what the law desires from you. The law does not desire to burden you or wound you. The law desires to lead you to your death. It will lead you straight to your own crucifixion.

~~~~~~~~~~~~~~~~~~~~

> "For all who rely on works of the law are under a curse; for it is written, 'Cursed be every one who does not abide by all things written in the book of the law, and do them'" (Galatians 3:10).

What is the curse?

"The soul that sins shall die" (Ezekiel 18:4).

~~~~~~~~~~~~~~~~~~~~

What we have hopefully learned up to this point is that our failures and weaknesses are God's useful tools. They lead us to our great need for God and His provision for us. What a perfect gift, then, was given to mankind through Moses so many years ago — the gift of the law. Surely nothing could do a better job of revealing our imperfections.

The law will do *for* you, what must be done *in* you. It will lead you to death. Its work is perfect. It excludes no one.

~~~~~~~~~~~~~~~~~~~~

> "...No man is justified before God by the law" (Galatians 3:11).

~~~~~~~~~~~~~~~~~~~~

By the law you will surely die; and, just as surely, you will experience the grace of God as never before. I invite you to go with me, in the next few chapters, down the path on which the law of God will lead you. At road's end, you will find yourself at the feet of Jesus.

The Law:

I will not pretend to understand or love the law as I should. My thoughts on it come only from my experience with it. It has proven to be my friend. It was out of love that the law was given to us. We were given the law as a gift because it put us in a position of being able to obey God and reap the blessing and joy that comes from obedience. Jesus' greatest desire was and is to do the will of His Father. He knows the benefit that comes with obedience to His Father's will. What an incredible gift the law is that we can hope to obey it and thereby experience the abundant life that obedience brings.

God saw clearly, what we could not see. He saw that we were lost in a world of sin, and that we were unable to do what was right and pure. "There is none that does good, no not one" (Psalm 14:3). The biggest problem, however, is that we could not even determine what was good. Left to ourselves we could not discern right from wrong. The law, our custodian, was given to us in order that we could determine right from wrong, that we would know what is sin and what is not sin. "If it had not been for the law, I would not have known sin. I would not have known what it is to covet if the law had not said 'You shall not covet'" (Romans 7:7 NRSV).

A Good Christian:

Being a Christian and having been given the law, I set out to live by it. To obey! I wanted to be a good Christian. I had been doing pretty well at it too... living the Christian life. That is until one day when I deliberately chose to disobey. I did not just fail to obey; I chose to disobey. Somehow, it seemed very different. Choosing to do something that I knew was very much against God's will felt different than failing to do what I would have chosen to do. It was premeditated sin. I chose divorce.

Scripture taught me very clearly what God thought about my decision:

~~~~~~~~~~~~~~~~~~~~

> "And he said to them, 'Whoever divorces his wife and marries another, commits adultery against her, and if she divorces her husband and marries another, she commits adultery'" (Mark 10:11).

~~~~~~~~~~~~~~~~~~~~

How can this be?! I had never done anything that even smelled like adultery. I was a good Christian living a good Christian life, trapped in a horrible marriage.

~~~~~~~~~~~~~~~~~~~~

> "Every one who divorces his wife and marries another commits adultery, and he who marries a woman divorced from her husband commits adultery" (Luke 16:18).

~~~~~~~~~~~~~~~~~~~~

I chose divorce. In so doing I was making an adulterer of myself, and if there ever were to come a time when I should remarry I would make an adulterer out of the person who would marry me. Ouch!

This is what I chose. It was all very clear. Scripture does not leave much room for discussion on this issue. No "if onlys" or "yah buts." My decision left me numb. If only my situation had fallen into one of the loopholes of the law!

Loopholes ???:

Matthew 19 seemingly provides a loophole. In the case of unchastity or unfaithfulness, I am off the hook. "And I say to you: whoever divorces his wife, *except for unchastity*, and marries another, commits adultery" (Matthew 19:9, italics added). That sure looks like a loophole. In 1 Corinthians, I find what appears to be another loophole. "But if the unbelieving partner desires to separate, let it be so; in such a case the brother or sister is not bound" (1 Corinthians 7:15). And of course, there is the ultimate loophole — death. "Thus a married woman is bound by the law to her husband as long as he lives; but if her husband dies, she is discharged from the law concerning the husband" (Romans 7:2 NRSV). There were three loopholes that I believed could get me off the hook.

The problem was that my marriage did not fit into one of those loopholes. As horrible and rotten as my situation was, I could not find anything in Scripture that would get me off the hook. So, all I could do was stay in the marriage and hope that one day my husband would either leave me, be unfaithful to me, or drop dead. Then, I thought, it would be O.K., because then I would be Biblically off the hook.

<u>Finally!:</u>

My all-knowing, all-loving God knew this about me. He knew that I had this shallow concept of who He was. God knew that I had this deep misunderstanding of the law and its intent. He graciously left me to make this decision with no loophole protection. As a result, all I could do was throw myself down at the feet of Jesus and say, "Do with me what You will." I knew I was completely deserving of whatever punishment came my way. I was unable even to beg for mercy. I was guilty. (Mind you, at the time I thought I was guilty for getting the divorce, not for hoping he would drop dead.) Nonetheless, it took this incident in my life to bring me to the point where I lay utterly broken before God. There was no merit left in me. There was no delusion about what a good Christian I was.

During those five years of marriage I had grown to love my Lord more than anything else. I had experienced Him in ways that I never had in my previous years as a Christian. He was my all in all. It was against Him that I was deliberately choosing to sin. My own sin overwhelmed me.

~~~~~~~~~~~~~~~~~~~~

> "For I know my transgressions, and my sin is ever before me. Against thee, thee only, have I sinned, and done that which is evil in thy sight, so that thou art justified in thy sentence and blameless in thy judgment" (Psalm 51:3-4).

~~~~~~~~~~~~~~~~~~~~

It was at this point in my life that God was at last able to intervene with the truth. God gave me a glimpse into my heart and I saw the ugly truth that existed within me. I saw myself as a sinner.

At last the workings of the law had their full and necessary effect on me. The law is not something we as Christians can live by. It is something we will die by. We stand condemned because the law is here to point out our inability to live the life necessary for salvation. I stood before God guilty and in desperate need of His forgiving grace. The law revealed my sinfulness. The law revealed the truth about myself. The law is essential! The law led me to sin - sin brought death. "The soul that sins shall die" (Ezekiel 18:4). The law of sin and death had served its purpose in me. I was legally dead in sin. All I could do was lay myself down before God and wait to see how He would deal with me.

God's Response:

I opened my Bible and there I was — an adulterer:

~~~~~~~~~~~~~~~~~~~~

> "Early in the morning he came again to the temple; all the people came to him, and he sat down and taught them. The scribes and the Pharisees brought a woman who had been caught in adultery, and placing her in the midst they said to him, 'Teacher, this woman has been caught in the act of adultery. Now in the law Moses commanded us to stone such. What do you say about her? This they said to test him, that they might have some charge to bring against him. Jesus bent down and wrote with his finger on the ground. And as they continued to ask him, he stood up and said to them, 'Let him who is without sin among you be the first to throw a stone at her.' And once more he bent down and wrote with his finger on the ground. But when they heard it, they went away, one by one, beginning with the eldest, and Jesus was left alone with the women standing before him. Jesus looked
~~~~~~~~~~~~~~~~~~~~

> up and said to her, 'Woman, where are they? Has no one condemned you?' She said, 'No one, Lord.' And Jesus said, 'Neither do I condemn you; go, and do not sin again'" (John 8:2-11).

Jesus did not say, "Let him who is not an adulterer cast the first stone." He said, "Let him who is without sin cast the first stone." And then, Jesus, the one who alone was without sin, did not throw a stone at me. God opened my eyes to my sinfulness so that I was then free to experience His grace. I experienced an entirely new dimension of His grace.

What a beautiful place it is, to be the one that is thrown down into the middle of a staring crowd, condemned by the law, only to look up and see the face of Jesus, ready to forgive. In fact, His grace towards me was ready to do far more than forgive. He was ready to renew. He desired to renew my life not simply to what it was prior to this experience. That would not be renewal at all. That would have put me back in utter darkness. He does not desire to *restore* any of us to spiritual blindness. He does desire to *renew* us to a right relationship with Him, an honest and truthful relationship. We can enjoy an intimate relationship with Jesus, living in constant fellowship with Him. No longer must we be cut off from Him due to our sinful blindness — blindness to our need for forgiveness — blind to the fact that every one of us needs to be thrown down into the dust before Christ, condemned as one who is with sin.

What I had failed to understand is that I was in that position all along. I simply did not see it. I did not understand that the very smallest of sins, even one, puts me in the same position as an adulterer or anyone else. My deliberate sin had no greater effect on my standing with God than did my simple sin of failing to live as I would choose. Sin is sin. My sin that was not premeditated did far more to keep me from God's grace because it kept me blind to the truth. I believe we will only experience the incredible, immeasurable grace of God in proportion to how clearly we see our sin.

Study Questions

Chapter Seven
Works

"The soul that sins shall die" (Ezekiel 18:4). Sin causes our spiritual death. Mankind's dilemma is that we are blind to sin, unable to discern right from wrong. We do not even know when we sin. Thus, God gave us a much-needed custodian. What custodian did God give us? ____________________. The law taught us right from wrong. The law does not desire to burden you or wound you. The law desires to lead you to your ____________________.

Many people, like myself, have been taught that the law is something we are to live by, and so we attempt to uphold the law. We believe that being a good Christian is contingent on how well we live by the rules. We have learned in previous chapters, however, that our problem is not an external problem it is ____________________.

We have an internal problem, and no amount of positive external behavior will produce an internal transformation.

The law is necessary in opening our eyes to our dilemma. What does the law help to reveal? ______________________________________

____

Having seen the truth about our condition, what does that free us up to experience? ____

____

Many of us forfeit the receiving of life through God's Holy Spirit for the life we are familiar with in the flesh. What is most familiar to you, living life in the flesh or living life in the Spirit? ___________

____

One way that we attempt to live the Christian life in the flesh is by trying to uphold the law. Make a list of some of the laws you have successfully lived by"

____

____

____

____

____

There are many times in each of our lives when we fail to obey God. Often, we do so unknowingly. What are some times when you may have unknowingly sinned against God? (i.e., sins we perceived as being "Part of the game.")

____

____

____

Have you ever deliberately sinned? Have you ever chosen to do something that you knew God did not want you to do?

____

____

"Let him who is without sin among you be the first to throw a stone at her" (John 8:7). Jesus could have thrown a stone at the adulterous woman we read about in scripture because He was without sin, but He did not. He knew the intention of the law then, and He still does today. The law takes you on a path that will ultimately leave you at the feet of Jesus. His grace is prepared to meet you there with the power to ________________ and ________________.

The perfect forgiveness that Jesus extends to us is overwhelming. But His grace is not limited to forgiveness alone. He also desires to renew us to all that He created us to be. The thing that Jesus wants more than anything is for each one of us to be renewed to a truthful and intimate relationship with our Father in heaven.

Does God restore us to the life we lived prior to our experience with the law? ____________________

What does He desire to renew us to? ____________________

Write about a time when you experienced Grace:

____

____

____

Imagine yourself being thrown into the midst of a crowd at the feet of Jesus. If you were to look into the face of Jesus, what do you think you would see? ____________________

____

Spend some time in prayer at the feet of Jesus...

Chapter Eight

Law and Grace

You will notice the title of this chapter is called Law *and* Grace, not Law *versus* Grace. It is not one or the other. There are many well-intentioned believers who feel that the law can now be abandoned because of the new covenant life we are able to experience through the provision of God's Holy Spirit. The law still serves an essential purpose. The law still must do its initial work of ushering us into that Spirit filled, graceful life.

Having experienced this incredible thing called forgiveness, God then begins teaching us about how these two things, law and grace, are brought together. The harshness of His law and the mercy of His love go hand in hand. He designed the perfect union between law and love.

> "For no human being will be justified in his sight by works of the law, since through the law comes knowledge of sin" (Romans 3:20). Why? "So that every mouth may be stopped, and all the world may become guilty before God" (Romans 3:19 KJV). "Law came in, to increase the trespass" (Romans 5:20). "If it had not been for the law, I would not have known sin. I would not have known what it is to covet if the law had not said 'You shall not covet'"

> (Romans 7:7 NRSV). Why the law? "In order that sin might be shown to be sin" (Romans 7:13).

~~~~~~~~~~~~~~~~~~~~

"No human being will be justified in his sight by works of the law" (Romans 3:20). Often, that is exactly what we try to do. We try to do what Romans 3:20 says is impossible to do. We try to justify ourselves by works of the law. We hold ourselves up to the law and we say to ourselves, "Hmm ... not bad. I'm looking pretty good, a few small misdemeanors that nobody even knows about. But, all in all, not bad."

<u>No Loopholes!:</u>

In the previous chapter I made reference to the loopholes that I believed existed in relation to marriage and divorce. That belief came out of my misunderstanding of the law. In light of the fact that the law is designed to reveal our sinfulness, it is important that we realize there are no loopholes within the law. Why would loopholes be provided if the goal is to reveal our sin and lead us to our death? Loopholes would be counterproductive to the desired outcome of the law. The purpose of the law never was and never will be to get you off the hook. Its purpose is to put you on it.

~~~~~~~~~~~~~~~~~~~~

> "You have heard that it was said, 'You shall not commit adultery. But I say to you that every one who looks at a woman lustfully has already committed adultery with her in his heart" (Matthew 5:27).

~~~~~~~~~~~~~~~~~~~

He wants us to make no mistake. He does not want to leave any room for confusion. When God opened my eyes to my sinfulness there was no more confusion in my mind. There was no "off the hook" for me. I'm hooked! I'm caught! I'm Guilty! I die!

Chapter one started out quoting Scripture from Luke 7:36-48. We were introduced to two people. One was a Pharisee who did
~~~~~~~~~~~~~~~~~~~

not see much need for God's forgiveness; the other was a sinner who saw very clearly her need for forgiveness. We learned from that passage that the person who is forgiven little, loves little.

How very grateful I am that I was temporarily blinded to the unfaithfulness of the man I chose to divorce. As God took me through the process of gently revealing to me the awful truth about what I am made of (my sinfulness), I had no idea of the infidelity that had been going on. It turns out that I had my loophole all along. How very grateful I am to God that He blinded me to anything that I would have grabbed on to in order to justify my own sin. I would have grabbed on to my husband's unfaithfulness as a loophole that would have legitimized my decision to divorce. As a result I might never have known what it is to be thrown in the dust before Jesus. I would have thought it was one of those O.K. times to get a divorce. How grateful I am that I was not prevented from experiencing the full intent of the law – condemnation. It's not that I wouldn't have been equally guilty before the law. No, I would have been equally guilty. I simply might not have seen the enormity of my guilt. He who is forgiven much, loves much. He who is forgiven little, loves little. I would have used the law to excuse me, not to condemn me.

<u>Deliberate Sin:</u>

Divorce is not the only way in which we choose to deliberately sin. It is only one of many. We have the opportunity to choose to do many things contrary to God's choosing. Coveting your friends house, abortion, not loving your neighbor as yourself, alternative lifestyles – they are all legal, socially acceptable, and common in our world today. I am only choosing to use divorce as an example because it is one that I had to seek God's guidance on.

I am not the first person who has taken up this issue with Jesus. The Pharisees took issue with Jesus on the topic of divorce. Let's look at what Jesus had to say...

~~~~~~~~~~~~~~~~~~~~

"And Pharisees came up and in order to test him asked, 'Is it lawful for a man to divorce his wife:'
~~~~~~~~~~~~~~~~~~~~

> He answered them, 'What did Moses command you?' They said, 'Moses allowed a man to write a certificate of divorce, and to put her away.' But Jesus said to them, 'For your hardness of heart he wrote you this commandment. But from the beginning of creation, 'God made them male and female.' 'For this reason a man shall leave his father and mother and be joined to his wife, and the two shall become one.' So they are no longer two but one. What therefore God has joined together, let not man put asunder" (Mark 10:2-9).

~~~~~~~~~~~~~~~~~~~~~~

When asked about divorce, Jesus went straight to the law. Jesus asked them, "What did Moses command you?" The Pharisees then pointed out that Moses allowed for divorce. Jesus' response to that was, "[It was] for your hardness of heart he wrote you this commandment." In other words, it is because of sin that allowances had to be made. This is not a positive concession making divorce right. This is not a loophole providing you a way out. This allowance is a judgment upon us. It is directed against us. It is evidence of our hardness of heart. Jesus uses the law to do what the law is designed to do, condemn us.

Jesus, having thus accused us of the sinfulness in our hearts, then goes straight to God's commandment. He goes from what is permitted in the Law of Moses to what is commanded by God. "But from the beginning of creation, 'God made them male and female.' For this reason a man shall leave his father and mother and be joined to his wife, and the two shall become one. What therefore God has joined together, let not man put asunder" (Mark 10:6-9).

Christ has just laid out the perfect intention of marriage. This is the only state of marriage that is acceptable to God. Nothing else is acceptable. Nothing. That is what Jesus has to say. Divorce happens when marriage does not happen. Divorce happens because of sin, the hardness of hearts. God's perfect plan, however, remains the same. It was the same yesterday and it will be the same tomorrow. His plan does not involve sin. God's plan does not make room for divorce.
~~~~~~~~~~~~~~~~~~~~~~

I have come to believe that every allowance that mankind has come up with has been provided because of the hardness of our hearts, because of sin. Every provision in the book of law is there because mankind's sinfulness requires that provision be made. It would be cruel and unjust for many people to have to remain within their marriages. I am grateful that my good friend, John, recognized mine as being one of them. But even these concessions in the law are a judgment against us. Please understand that I am not suggesting that divorce should never happen. Indeed, there are situations when a person should not remain in a marriage. Sin has deemed it necessary for concessions to be made. What I am suggesting is that it is necessary because of sin, not because it is right. Concessions are not loopholes. Concessions, like the law, point out our sin, not our righteousness. When something is the byproduct of sin it can never be right. You and I are born into this world as byproducts of generational sin, and we can never be right until Jesus makes us right by the power of His righteousness.

The law then, serves to make us guilty. When Scripture talks about what defiles a man in Matthew 15:19, it places evil thoughts before murder. Slander and false witness are listed alongside adultery and theft. There is no escape. The law is intent on finding you guilty.

When the Holy Spirit is working at drawing someone near to God, He will do so by making sin a very heavy burden. Sin will become an enormous weight to the one that is seeking after God. After a while the weight of sin will become unbearable. It is at this point that we are finally ready to be led down the pathway of law to the feet of Jesus. It is the only place where we will find someone ready and able to take our burden from us.

Will this burden of sin fall only on the non-Christian who is seeking for the truth? No. It will fall on all who need the refreshing renewal of the life God intends for us to live. There are many Christians who are saved, but not free. The freedom that God's grace brings is found at the end of the road on which His law will take you. Take that road and find the forgiveness that waits for you at the end of it. The healing balm of forgiveness and the awesome provision of God's grace will overwhelm you.

King David had been a Godly man for many years when he found himself at the feet of Jesus with the burden of his sin. The feet of Jesus is not, and should not be a place that we visit only one time. I believe that as Christians we do not spend enough time at the feet of Jesus in truth as we really are. May the day come for each one of us when we will cease to get up and walk away from that spot of forgiveness. What a glorious life it would be if we would stay right there with the constant reminder of who we are apart from God's forgiving grace. A place where we would always be ready to extend that grace to another — at the feet of Jesus!

Study Questions

Chapter Eight
Law and Grace

"No human being will be justified in his sight by works of the law, since through the law comes knowledge of sin" (Romans 3:20). "Since all have sinned and fall short of the glory of God, they are justified by his grace as a gift, through the redemption which is in Christ Jesus..." (Romans 3:23-24)

As Christians, we often try to justify ourselves by ____________

Can that be done? ____

What are we justified by? __________________________________

Because of mankind's hardness of heart, provision was made within the law. Does that provision justify our sinfulness?

____

This chapter teaches us that there are no __________________ within the law.

The law was given not in order to justify me, but rather to _______ ___________ me.
Loopholes would be counterproductive to that end.

Does the burden of sin fall only on a non-Christian? ___________

There are many Christians who are_________________, but not

____

Only as we experience God's grace personally will we taste the freedom that accompanies His grace. Until we experience grace from God we cannot extend it to another. Until we experience it, we can only attempt to imitate grace.

Can you think of a time in your life when you felt especially burdened by sin? ____

____

When the Holy Spirit convicts us, or burdens us with our sin, we may respond in one of two ways:

1) Go to God in truth with our sin offering and receive from Him forgiveness and renewal.
2) Become comfortable with our sin. Deny it as being sin and accept it as normal.

The Holy Spirit is attempting to lead us to freedom by the power of conviction. If we ignore His prompting we will all too quickly grow complacent in our sin.

Rabbi Yitzhak writes, "At first, sin is like an occasional visitor, then like a guest who stays for awhile, and finally like the master of the house."[6]

What people come to your mind when you think of sin becoming master of the house? ____

____

It is easy to look outside of ourselves and see the sins of others. Can you see any areas in your life where you may have once struggled with gnawing feelings of conviction, but have managed to push those feelings aside? (i.e., neglecting relationships, addictive behaviors)

____

____

Prayer: There have been times, Lord, when I have indeed used the law to justify my sin. I have used the law to reveal my goodness not my sinfulness. I have attempted to live by the law not realizing that to enter into that kind of relationship with the law immediately brings death, not life. Allow the law to serve its purpose in me. Reveal to me that which only You can reveal. Help me to view conviction as a friend and not an enemy. Teach me what it is to enter into a new covenant relationship with You. Holy Jesus, I desire to escape from the law of sin and death. Accept me now, Lord, as one who has fully entered into a new relationship with You through the law of the Spirit of life. Holy Spirit, fill me with freedom. Holy Spirit, thank You that You dwell within me! The curtain is torn! I have become the Holy of Holies. Holy Father, You have made forgiveness and renewal possible through Your Son, because of Your enormous love for me – Hallelujah! Amen.

Chapter Nine

The Church

As individuals we come to know God's grace only as we see our need for it. We will not have grace to offer others until we experience the power of God's forgiveness in our own lives. The corporate body of Christians, the church, will only come to know God's grace as that grace is experienced and expressed through each individual. Many local churches beautifully demonstrate God's grace to others through those graceful individuals. There are many individuals, however, that do not demonstrate grace, instead they hold on to the law. As a result, many churches are governed and represented by individuals who do not yet have grace to give. We must begin, therefore, by extending grace to those who do not have grace to extend in return. It is easy to forget that we were that person not too long ago. Having said that, let us look at the impact the church's lack of grace can have on the wounded sinner who so desperately longs to find forgiveness.

<u>A Law-Abiding Church:</u>

> "For the law of the Spirit of Life in Christ Jesus has set me free from the law of sin and death" (Romans 8:2).

It grieves my heart when I think of the many churches that are built on a foundation of the law of sin and death, rather than the law of the Spirit of Life. The first law leads only to death, the latter leads to life. It saddens me greatly to see churches attempting to define the law in order to set boundaries by which they will measure an individual's worthiness. My heart aches for all who find themselves outside of those boundaries. In too many churches those hurting people become useless outcasts.

In no way am I suggesting that we not judge the sinful behavior. It is essential that we recognize sin and call it what it is. Indeed, we must not only judge the sinful behavior, we must also attach to the one who committed the sin his deserved punishment. "The soul that sins shall die" (Ezekiel 18:4). Sin is not something to take lightly. The law of the Spirit requires judgment of the sin and the sinner. We can never arrive at this new law of the Spirit without the legal law. We sin, therefore, we are deserving of death.

The difference between the legal law and the law of the Spirit is that the legal law stops at condemnation. The legal law judges the sin, and condemns the sinner. That is the end result of the legal law. The law of the Spirit starts out on exactly the same course as the legal law. The difference is that it does not stop at condemnation. The end result of the legal law (death) is then met with the overwhelming possibility that can come through the law of the Spirit of life. The possibility of new life comes to us through the power of forgiveness and renewal. God renews us to a life full of purpose and meaning. God raised up the most unlikely characters to further His kingdom. Tax collectors, murderers, and prostitutes were all listed among Jesus' closest friends and together they worked side by side.

Today is no different; you can be certain that God does not forgive and renew so that a person can be exiled from leadership within the church for the rest of their life. On the contrary, these outcasts are the very people that God will raise up to lead, because they will know the way to grace. The person who finds their way to grace will know that grace is not found within the confines of the legal law. There are, sadly, many churches that attempt to incorporate grace within the legal law. They do so by defining and redefining the law.

CHURCH A
Women cover your heads. Women be silent in the church. Only men may teach. Divorced men may not be in leadership.

CHURCH B
A woman's hair is her covering. Women may teach women or children. Women may team with their spouse in a mixed setting. Women may be Deacons but not Elders. A divorced person may be in leadership if their situation falls within the loopholes of the law.

Both of these churches live by the law. The first box is attempting to hold to every letter of the law. They have used Scripture to define the law. The second box has decided to make room for what they consider to be God's grace. They interpret Scripture in such a way that allows them to make the box bigger. In truth, they have simply redefined the law.

When we attempt to bring grace into a structure that is based on, and lives by law, we are not living by grace at all. Such an attempt is nothing more that a cheap imitation of grace. When God is limited in what He can do with any human life, we have not entered the realm of grace, regardless of how big we make the box.

Grace cannot be measured in an external way. Grace is not determined by the presence, or absence, of rules. When grace is absent the problem is not an external one, it is internal. Grace does not look at how well you stay within the confines of the box. Grace knows you have already failed at staying within the true confines of the law. Grace condemns you from the start and then waits for you to realize that you have failed to live by the law. Grace looks at one thing — your heart. A church that lives by grace will concern itself with one thing — your heart.

~~~~~~~~~~~~~~~~~~~~

Frank fell out of the confines of the box. He left his wife and two kids for another woman. There was no loophole protection for Frank. Frank blew it! Frank suffered for many years under the weight of his sinful decision, not believing that God could, or would, ever forgive him for his terrible mistake. Today, Frank has discovered God's forgiveness and God's renewal. Frank has a broken and contrite heart. Frank has experienced grace.

~~~~~~~~~~~~~~~~~~~~

Sam believes he has spent his life within the confines of the box. Although he would never tell you, he is just a little bit proud of that. Sam had to explain to Frank that he could not hold a position of leadership in the church because of his past. "Some things," Sam said, "just cannot be undone."

~~~~~~~~~~~~~~~~~~~~

I do not worry about Frank; he will be okay. He will humbly accept the consequences of his past sin. God can always pull Frank from this church and put him into a graceful environment where he will be a blessing to others. No, Frank is not who I worry about. It is the church that I worry about.

Sam's church will, no doubt, pray for God's provision and direction. Unfortunately, they will probably turn away many people that God would provide. When the qualification for leadership is
~~~~~~~~~~~~~~~~~~~~

measured by external criteria we run great risk of not accepting God's provision, because God's criteria will not be external, they will be internal. He looks at our heart.

God desires that we repent. He wants us to see our sin, turn from our sin, and desire to sin no more. When we hate sin, then we are developing a heart like that of our Savior. Can you begin to see the necessity of conviction? There can be no repentance where there is no conviction.

Grace does not eliminate the need for accountability. Grace does not hold the door wide open for sin to enter in. Grace slams the door on sin. While the imperfect Law of Moses helps us by naming sin, it leaves us without the power to see it, own it, and rid ourselves of it. It leaves us dead in our sin.

While there are many churches that err by remaining slaves to the law of sin and death, so are there many churches that err by allowing sin to be dismissed entirely. Many churches err on the side of license. To live by grace does not mean that you live by what the world today calls tolerance. Tolerance is not grace! Grace does not give us license to sin. Grace condemns sin.

There can be no grace apart from conviction and condemnation. The heart must first experience conviction and condemnation in order for it to be ushered into the realm of grace. Grace is about forgiveness and renewal. Tolerance has no need of forgiveness and renewal, because tolerance does not convict or condemn. Tolerance simply accepts the sin.

A Matter of the Heart:

It is one thing for grace to happen *to* a person, it is another thing when the power of grace happens *within* a person. It is the difference of being the recipient of another person's graciousness and being the giver of grace. Such a difference becomes a matter of the heart. God looks at the heart of each individual. He knows the truth about what is in each heart and mind. He desires that we, too, concern ourselves with the heart of each individual. The Spirit of God does not provide us with a foolproof list of prerequisites that we can use in determining a person's qualifications for leadership. The Spirit of

God sets us free from that list. It provides something much greater and more powerful. It provides us with wisdom and discernment, in order that we may judge not the deeds of a person, but the heart of a person. While the condition of the heart may be evidenced by external behaviors (whether good or bad), it is not the external behaviors or deeds that we are looking to judge, it is the heart from which those deeds spring. Negative external behaviors may not always point to a hardened heart, and positive external behaviors may not always point to a heart given over to God. It requires discernment to see matters of the heart, such as pride and a self-righteous attitude, or sorrow and repentance.

This is a difficult concept to put into words because there is so much room for misunderstanding. Please know that I am not suggesting a careless acceptance of any individual into leadership regardless of their past. It is only the sinner that has experienced the power of grace *within* that may grow into a position to lead. In time, that person may be raised up to lead as a discerning giver of grace. To offer a position of leadership to someone with a history of sin that has not yet been crushed and renewed by the Spirit of God would not be wise. Wisdom and discernment are part of what God graciously provides when we ask. Many of us don't trust the *asking*. We fear that God will not be able to give us the wisdom we need to make choices of who should lead, and it is, therefore, much easier to have a checklist that will tell us who is qualified and who is not.

Law is one thing - grace is another thing. I have emphasized the need for both law and grace. Too often, churches, instead of embracing these two separate gifts in their fullness, will try to pour a little bit of grace into their structure of law. Trying to mix grace in with the law is like trying to mix oil and water. It cannot be done. I much prefer that a church that decides to live by the law would keep the box small. Those who stretch the box by redefining the law are only deceiving themselves, and many of my brothers and sisters in Christ, into believing that grace is something that it is not. Satan must love it when we make living in the law look attractive because then we will be content to live within it. If we are content to live within the law, we will never seek after and know the truth about God's grace.

A Graceful Church:

A graceful church cannot be defined. A church governed by grace is led by the Spirit, and the Spirit's leading cannot be defined. I cannot draw a box for you that will show you what a Spirit-led church looks like, because each church will be unique unto itself.

You might ask, "How does a church move from law into grace?" The answer can only be, "One individual at a time." When the law has served its purpose and led an individual to its desired end, death, then that one individual is in a position to experience grace. For that one individual grace becomes reality. A life of grace can only be arrived at when the law has served its purpose. When grace is thrown in prior to the law having achieved its purpose in us, it is not grace. There cannot be resurrected life prior to death. Death leads to life.

~~~~~~~~~~~~~~~~~~~~

> "Truly, truly, I say to you, unless a grain of wheat falls into the earth and dies, it remains alone; but if it dies, it bears much fruit. He who loves his life loses it, and he who hates his life in this world will keep it for eternal life" (John 12:4-25).

~~~~~~~~~~~~~~~~~~~~

When we hate the sin that represents our lives we are ready to lose our life to God. In our desperation we become dependent on God. God is finally able to teach us that our merit is not our own, and apart from Him we can do nothing. When we at last die to who we are apart from God, we will become all that He created us to be. He calls Himself our Father, and He created us to be His children, alive and free, able to receive and give love through His life-giving Spirit.

We are now free to live outside of the custodial care of the law. We have been set free from the curse of death that goes along with living by the law.

~~~~~~~~~~~~~~~~~~~~

> "For all who rely on works of the law are under a curse; for it is written, 'Cursed be every one who does not abide by all things written in the book of the law, and do them'" (Galatians 3:10).
>
> "Christ redeemed us from the curse of the law..." (Galatians 3:13a).
>
> "Now before faith came, we were confined under the law, kept under restraint until faith should be revealed. So that the law was our custodian until Christ came, that we might be justified by faith. But now that faith has come, we are no longer under a custodian; for in Christ Jesus you are all sons of God, through faith" (Galatians 3: 23-26).

~~~~~~~~~~~~~~~~~~~~

Faith has come! Listen to what faith brought with it when it came to us....

~~~~~~~~~~~~~~~~~~~~

> "There is neither Jew nor Greek, there is neither slave nor free, there is neither male nor female; for you are all one in Christ Jesus" (Galatians 3:28).

~~~~~~~~~~~~~~~~~~~~

Grace breaks down every barrier. Grace takes away all of the external roadblocks of race, social status, and gender. We are all one in Christ Jesus. As individuals begin to live free of those barriers then the church will begin to recognize and receive God's leading and God's provision.

A graceful Church will be made up of graceful individuals. There is no other way for a graceful Church to exist. Those who find comfort in the law will not find comfort in a graceful environment. We cannot look for the church to change outside of ourselves. We can only look to God in order that in Him we may experience this thing called Grace.

We are the church, you and I. As you and I experience grace through our personal and intimate relationship with Jesus, then you and I will walk, live, and breathe in that grace. It will be yours. Others will see it in you and experience it through you — but it will not be theirs until they find themselves at the feet of Jesus.

Study Questions

Chapter Nine
The Church

Should *any* person who has been involved in a life of sin be invited to be a spiritual leader in the church? ______________________

Should *any* person who has lived a stain free life, seemingly within the confines of the law, be invited to be a spiritual leader in the church? ______________________________________

Examining a person's past record, be it blemished or unblemished, will not help in determining whether or not they would make a good candidate for spiritual leadership.

It is not external criteria, in and of itself, that qualifies or disqualifies an individual in relation to how God can use them in the body of Christ. The problem with any individual will always be ________ ____________ not external.

God looks at our ____________________.

While the condition of the heart may be evidenced by external behaviors, it is not the external behaviors or deeds we are looking to judge, it is the heart from which those deeds spring.

God desires that we _______________________ our sin, and ____________________.

"A broken and contrite heart, O God thou wilt not despise" (Psalm 51:17b).

"For the tree is known by its fruit" (Matthew 12:33b).

How do we know the heart of a person? ___________________

God provides us with _________________ and _____________.

We must ask God for these things. He desires that we ask, because He desires to give them. They are part of His provision to us.

"If any of you lacks wisdom, let him ask God, who gives to all men generously and without reproaching, and it will be given him" (James 1:5).

Does Grace give us license to sin? ______________________
Grace hates sin! Grace has the power not only to expose sin, but also to deal with that sin to its completion.
The end result of the legal law is ______________________
The end result of grace is ______________________ and ____

Think about various leaders we know about in the Bible. What was God concerned about in each of these lives? Write about some examples:
____
____
____

How does a church begin to move from being a lawful church, to a graceful church? ______________________________
____

Be patient with others, as God has been patient with you. Do not hold others accountable for what God reveals to you. It is your eyes He has opened to that truth. God will bless your life with that truth and He will teach you how to bless others with it. Pray that God will do His work in each member of your particular church body. Only God can reveal truth, you cannot! Pray that you will have spiritual ears to hear and spiritual eyes to see. Pray that you will be one through whom He may love others and show others what grace looks like, so that they will see it and desire it.

Prayer: Help me to see more clearly, Father. Open my eyes to the truth as You desire for me to see it. Thank You that I have experienced Your grace from within. Raise me up, now, to be a dispenser of grace. You have forgiven me. I am now able to forgive others. Build Your church, not just in number, but also in power. Give us the power to love.

Part Two

Resurrected Life

"… and whoever loses his life for my sake will find it."
Mathew 16:25

Chapter Ten

Agree And Be Free

Crucified by Truth:

When we see ourselves in truth, this mysterious concept of our being crucified becomes clear. We are crucified by truth. The truth is that we are not right (righteous). Christ saves us because we need saving. This crucifixion does not necessarily happen when we first believe and accept Jesus as Savior. When we first invite Jesus Christ to come into our lives and accept Him as our Savior we do not always grasp the enormity of our problem (sinfulness). For many, that is when we believe Jesus is who He says He is, but we do not see clearly who we are. When we accept His gift of salvation we become "saved sinners." Unfortunately, while we are quick to appropriate the "saved" part of our new identity, we are also somewhat quick to rid ourselves of the "sinner" part. This quick transition sometimes causes us to go from a position of unrighteousness to one of self-righteousness. We begin to lose sight of our sinful potential and focus instead on our ability to be good. Understanding our self-righteous beliefs does not occur apart from God revealing that truth to us. Seeing clearly the truth about our sinful selves will help bring us to the end of ourselves. It is then that we will experience Jesus as Lord.

David did not truly die to his own goodness until God sent Nathan to point out his sinfulness. Peter did not truly die until he saw the truth about his own weakness. Moses was a mighty man until he realized his capability to commit murder. Until we come face to face with what we are truly made of, this death experience cannot be our reality. The Pharisees' hearts were far from God because they focused on their goodness, their own righteousness. Focusing on our goodness will keep us from finding our way to resurrected living. Until God opens our eyes, like He did for David, we will not be able to approach God with a broken heart. Oh how David suffered when he finally understood the magnitude of his sin, and oh how beautifully he reveals his heart, not only to God, but to all of us...

~~~~~~~~~~~~~~~~~~~~

> "Have mercy on me, O God, According to thy steadfast love; according to thy abundant mercy blot out my transgressions. Wash me thoroughly from my iniquity, and cleanse me from my sin! For I know my transgressions, and my sin is ever before me. Against thee, thee only, have I sinned, and done that which is evil in thy sight, so that thou art justified in thy sentence and blameless in thy judgment" (Psalms 51:1-4).

~~~~~~~~~~~~~~~~~~~~

God truly is justified in the sentence and judgment He gives us. His sentence is death. "The soul that sins shall die" (Ezekiel 18:4). We are guilty. Agreement with that fact is the only place to start. The more clearly we see our sin, the more honestly we can go before God with our sin. This is the first and most essential thing that truth desires to reveal to us. It is how we find our way to God's love. I cannot emphasize enough the importance of this. It is the pathway to freedom. The truth will set you free.

Resurrected by Truth:

Seeing myself in truth allowed me to begin to see others in truth. Prior to this revelation of truth it was impossible to see how others' sinful behavior related to me. Prior to God opening my eyes to the fact that I am indeed made of flesh and bone and sin, I could see two sides — guilty and not guilty, perpetrator and victim. Now, I can look at the sinful offense and respond with, "That person is the same as me, for I am equally capable of committing the same offense." There is only one side - guilty, and we are all on the same side.

We begin to expect from others the very same thing we would expect from ourselves apart from God's revelation of truth in us. Apart from God's truth working life in us, we can expect very little. Agreeing with God about my condition makes it possible for me to agree with God about your condition as well. Apart from God, we both stand hopelessly in need. Agree and be free. Free to see things more clearly. Free to extend grace to the offender. It becomes possible to replace judgment and condemnation with grace.

If you have not yet agreed with God about how things are, this would be a good time to do it. Agree with God about the problem you and I were born into, the problem of sin. The solution to the problem is this: Lay yourself down before God in truth as you really are and invite Him to do with you what He will. It will be at that point that you will experience a new dimension of God's grace. He will teach you there is nothing you can do to make yourself right with Him. You are hopelessly stuck in a place of condemnation. That is why God made a plan to save you.

God sent His Son to do what you could not do - Jesus lived a sinless life. Jesus offered up to the highest court in the universe His perfect life in place of yours. He was sentenced with your deserved punishment. Jesus went to hell. You do not have to go to hell; your slate is clean when you accept His gift. Accept it and say "thank you." If ever "thank you" did not seem like enough this might be the time. Say it anyway.

We might think it is enough that Jesus saves us from hell for all eternity. But it is not all He gives us. There's more! He wants us to experience resurrected life. Resurrected life is possible because Jesus conquered death, the gates of hell could not keep Him. Jesus returned from the dead in order to offer us still more. He wants to empower us with the Spirit of God; the very Spirit that conquered death. He will do that through the power of truth. Truth desires to expose and put to death the lies that we live by. The first lie to be crucified is the lie of our own righteousness (self-righteousness). When we see ourselves in truth as we really are, then we are at last ready to experience resurrected life.

The Spirit of truth can now begin to work its transforming miracle of life within us. While transformation does not happen all at once, crucifixion can remain our daily blessing as we continue to allow the Spirit of truth to expose the many lies that we still hold dear. Give yourself to Him daily. Ask Him to teach you and speak to you. Allow Him to comfort you and guide you. His truth will work in you the miracle of transformation. You will not be transformed by willpower and determination. You will be transformed by the Spirit of truth. As the Spirit of truth is given the opportunity to have His way in your life, you will grow increasingly in love with your Savior, Jesus, and you will increasingly experience a life of love lived out from within you.

The Christian Life:

When we have found ourselves at the feet of Jesus, condemned and sentenced, then we are finally at the place where Jesus wants us to be. It is a place where we experience true humility. Not humiliation, but humility. Humiliation is self-centered; it attacks our self-esteem, lowering our self-image. Humility exists when our self-image cannot be lowered because it has found secure footing in the truthful perspective of who we are in Christ. At the feet of Jesus humility sees truthfully and understands that it is not about experiencing undeserved or unfair treatment. That is how humiliation sees life. Those unfair or undeserved humiliations will wound our self-image. Humility will allow our focus to look beyond ourselves — beyond our need to protect our self-image. From a position of humility we can approach life with a heart that is more like Jesus. Jesus is gentle and lowly of heart. The sweet, healing taste of humility will at last empower us to live the Christian life — if only for today.

This enormous privilege of dying before Jesus is an opportunity we have every day of our earthly lives. Like Paul we may "die every day" so that the Spirit of God may live. This death experience cannot be maintained apart from our holding onto a clear perspective of God's truth. Our seeing the truth allows God to live through us. The truth will keep us gentle and lowly of heart (humble). It is the gentle and lowly of heart that become able to live the supernatural life that bears witness to Christ. It is a life of God's Spirit being lived out in us. Either He will live through us or we will live life our own way and in our own strength. We can keep trying on our own. We can try yet another formula that promises to be the key to successful Christian living. When that formula fails we can try another formula, and then another, and another, until we become tired. In our exhaustion we will hopefully realize there is no formula, there is only death. Crucifixion leads to resurrected life. It is a difficult truth to arrive at — the truth that you can't do it.

Apart from the Holy Spirit no amount of reading the Bible, going to church, or fellowshipping with Christians will empower you to live a resurrected life. While these are all very important things, unless the Spirit of God breathes truth and life into them, they will simply be religious activities. God's Spirit must teach us as we read the Bible, His Spirit must equip us to serve in the church, His Spirit must empower us to love others as we fellowship with them. God alone can do these things. He alone can do it through us. Many Christians attempt to give meaning and purpose to their Christian walk by working hard in the church, or studying, or teaching. These are wonderful things when they are motivated and empowered by God. When these things are empowered by God it is called "service." When they are done apart from that power it is called "works." Too much work will only make you tired. (We will look more closely at this concept in future chapters.)

Nothing will give meaning to your life except the personal revelation and knowledge of Jesus Christ. This is not head knowledge, but personal knowledge that allows you to say, "I know Him." Decide now to drop everything that takes your time away from that which you are attempting to move towards — intimacy with Jesus. Seek after Him with all your heart. Make knowing Him your primary pursuit.

Do you want to experience the freedom of the Christian life? Then you must experience the Spirit of God empowering you to live that life. Christ alone is able to live the Christian life. You cannot live the Christian life apart from the Spirit of God. What freedom! — To realize that all the hard work you have lived under can come to an end. Stop trying to do it. You can't. Instead, ask the Spirit that lives in you to reveal Christ to you. And then, watch and see what the Christian life looks like. As you begin to see and experience the power of His love, you will desire to be like Him. You will begin to live the Christian life from a desire to be like Christ and not from willpower. We will see that the Christian life is not simply about what He *did*, it is about who He *is*. The Holy Spirit will reveal the inner life of Jesus, the heart of the man, not the deeds of the man. We can begin to experience the heart of Jesus in us because we are the very dwelling place of the Spirit of God. We can experience the miracle of gentleness and lowliness.

~~~~~~~~~~~~~~~~~~~~

When Adam was fashioned out of clay, God breathed into him and Adam began to take in air. When the Spirit of God is born in us, once again He breathes into us and we learn that air does not give life — the Spirit of God gives life. We are started on a journey that takes us out of the natural realm and puts us on a supernatural course. His Spirit will transform us.
~~~~~~~~~~~~~~~~~~~~

Study Questions

Chapter Ten
Agree And Be Free

We are crucified by the ___________________.

Why do we need saving? _________________________________
____

When we first invite Jesus Christ to come into our lives and accept Him as our Savior we do not always grasp the enormity of our problem. What is our problem? ___________________________________
For many, we accept Christ because we believe Jesus is who He says He is, but we do not see clearly who we are.
When we accept His gift of salvation we become "saved sinners." Unfortunately, while we are quick to appropriate the "___________ _____" part of our new identity, we are also somewhat quick to rid ourselves of the "________________" part. This quick transition sometimes causes us to go from a position of unrighteousness to one of ___________-______________________. We begin to lose sight of our sinful potential and focus instead on our ability to be good.

We may find ourselves seeing people as being either guilty or not guilty; when in truth there is only one side, __________________, and we are all on the same side.

We are often amazed when someone commits a sin, as though it were shocking or unusual for such a thing to happen. When we see in truth what we are made out of, it becomes much easier to understand why sin runs rampant in the lives of people. While we often shake our heads in disgust at other people's sinful behavior, it seldom truly offends us unless the sin is committed directly against us. When you or I become the recipient of a wrongdoing, then the sin becomes enormous.

When I look at the sins of others, it makes it easy for me to lose sight of my own potential to sin. There seems to be a direct correlation between my sins growing smaller as I view someone else's as growing bigger.

What sin has been committed against you that has been difficult for you to forgive? ____

____

Are you waiting for the person who committed that sin to make things right? ____

Has someone else's behavior caused you to experience the bondage of unforgiveness? ____________________________________

____

My sin is ____
My offender's sin is ______________________________________
How do we differ? ____

It is not our job to *make* others see their sinfulness (only God can do that), but rather, it is for us to be aware of our own potential to sin.

Jesus responds to our treatment of Him with the offer of salvation and the gift of His life-giving Spirit.

~~~~~~~~~~~~~~~~~~~~

> "Come to me, all who labor and are heavy laden, and I will give you rest. Take my yoke upon you, and learn from me, for I am gentle and lowly in heart, and you will find rest for your souls. For my yoke is easy, and my burden is light" (Matthew 11:28-30).

~~~~~~~~~~~~~~~~~~~~

In this verse, what are the two character qualities that describe Jesus?
________________ and ______________________________________

When we are confronted with our sin before Jesus, we are at last in a position to learn from Him what it is to be gentle and lowly in heart. We will experience humility.
Unforgiveness is a heavy burden. Humility begins to lighten our burden.

The Holy Spirit lives within the Christian. For you and me, the supernatural can become natural. Forgiveness can be a reality!

Prayer: Dear Jesus, I can only agree. I agree with You that I am guilty and desperately in need of Your grace. Do with me what You will. It is against You that I have sinned. I have responded to You with unforgiveness and self-centeredness. It is my own sin that has wounded me. Thank You that You have revealed the truth to me, so that I can lay myself down before You today in truth. I ask for Your forgiveness. Thank You that You forgive me. Thank You that You offer me a new life. I accept Your gift. Please teach me what that new life can look like. Teach me how to respond to those who, like me, have sinned against You. Holy Spirit, allow me to experience in my heart the supernatural reality of forgiveness toward those who have hurt me.

Chapter Eleven

Free To Ask

When you invite Jesus Christ to come into your heart as Savior and Lord, there is a new birth that takes place within you. It is the birth of a new spirit, the Holy Spirit, in the inner most part of your being. He takes up residency in your life and He will never leave you. The Bible talks about this opportunity we have to invite Jesus into our lives. In Revelations 3:20 Jesus says, "I stand at the door and knock; if anyone hears my voice and opens the door, I will come into him...." In other words, He stands ready, but He waits for an invitation. He does not stand at the door with a railroad tie and say, "Move over — I'm coming in on the count of three." He does not force Himself on you.

God has given you something that sets you apart from all other living creatures. It is part of what makes you "in the image of God." It is called a free will. You can choose God or you can reject Him.

<u>Boundaries:</u>

As a psychotherapist one of my goals is to teach healthy boundary-setting to my clients. Boundary-setting is a fundamental building block to a successful, fulfilling life. The simplicity of boundary-setting causes us to almost overlook it:

~~~~~~~~~~~~~~~~~~~~

You are responsible for your thoughts, feelings, beliefs, behaviors, choices, needs, and values. In relation to adults, you are not responsible for anyone else's. You are responsible **to** *the people that your boundaries impact, but you are not responsible* **for** *other people's boundaries. "You are responsible to others and for yourself."* [7]

~~~~~~~~~~~~~~~~~~~~

That was it. You may want to go back and read that again.

I am responsible *to* my husband in relation to my boundaries. If I choose to go out with my girlfriends for dinner, I will respectfully let my husband know about that choice. I am not responsible for my husband's boundaries. If he decides to go camping with his buddies, that is his decision. Because our choices impact each other's lives, we share a belief that causes us to want to check with each other before making a choice that will affect each other's world.

Our personal boundaries make up our free will. It is a precious thing God has given us. Having been made in the image of God, we have a free will that makes us fully responsible for our personal boundaries. We are to guard our boundaries. Why? Because of the tremendous harm that can come to others and ourselves when we do not. Relationships get into trouble when one of two things happen. 1) When someone forfeits their boundary and lets someone else decide what they should think, feel, believe, or choose; or 2) When an individual stomps on someone else's boundary, telling them what they will do, think, or choose. Either scenario is destructive to relationships.

For example, if Sharon wants to go out with her girlfriends and her husband reminds her of a prior commitment, she can thank him for reminding her and decide accordingly. If her husband simply wants to control her life and forbids her from going out with the girls so that she can stay home and fix him dinner, then she is put in a position where she must either decide to forfeit her boundary for the sake of peace, or go out anyway and prevent her husband from controlling her life in an unhealthy way. If she allows her husband that control she is making way for bitterness and resentment to build.

While going out with her friends may feel like an act of rebellion or disrespect, it is often a necessary step in creating a healthy relationship. The disruption caused by her choice may bring immediate turmoil to the relationship. In the long run, it will hopefully set a precedent that leads to the healthy respect of personal boundaries. Her goal is not to send a message that says, "I don't care what you think, I'm going out anyway." Her goal is to send a message that says, "I do care what you think. Therefore, I want you to know that I love you and my choosing to go out is not about wanting to hurt you, it is about wanting to nurture those friendships."

If John wants to go out bowling with the guys, he may need to discern why his wife does not want him to go. Are her reasons valid and helpful, or does she have an unhealthy hold on her husband's boundaries. I am sure you all know someone who has the "my way or the highway mentality." That person is the one who will err on the side of stomping on another's boundaries. I'm sure you also know someone who forfeits their choices and opinions to the person who is successfully controlling those boundaries. It is easy to forfeit a choice or opinion in the face of such pressure. To forfeit a boundary is not healthy, neither is it healthy to control or manipulate another's boundary.

Until we assume a healthy responsibility for our boundaries, we will all have a tendency to either forfeit or control. Based on our strengths, weaknesses, spiritual gifts, or past wounds, we will either be more susceptible to forfeiting our boundaries or wanting to control other's boundaries. Perhaps you already see yourself falling into one of these two categories. It is important to know which is our vulnerability – forfeiture or control. Only then can we be aware of and attempt to change any unhealthy patterns.

A third alternative, that of respecting each other's boundaries, offers the healthy exchange of give and receive. Giving is not forfeiture, and receiving is not taking. Influencing each other's worlds is essential to a healthy relationship. Controlling each other's worlds will prevent a healthy relationship.

In a healthy exchange, even if Sharon would like to go out with her friends, she may chose to stay home. Perhaps her husband is home sick or she hasn't spent much time with him lately. Rather than forfeit her boundary, she may choose to give the gift of time to her husband. If John knows his wife would freely send him off to go camping with his buddies, he may then choose to go or not go. He may decline, without feeling controlled by her, in order to spend time with her over the weekend. He will also have the option to go camping with his wife's blessing. If, on the other hand, either Sharon or John were adamant in not allowing the other to make their own choice, then neither would be in a position to give or receive from the other.

God models boundary-setting in His relationship with each one of us. Not once has God forced you or me to behave a certain way, or believe a certain thing. He has never taken over our list of boundaries, saying, "I'm God, today I will bypass your free will! I am going to make you believe in me!" I am certain there are times when He would like to. There are certainly consequences for the choices we make. As a rule, healthy choices will reap positive consequences and unhealthy, or poor, choices will reap negative consequences. None-the-less we are always left with choice.

There are many Old Testament stories that at first glance may look like God is taking over someone's boundaries and forcing His way. A second look may help us to see that God Himself, the one with the power to strip man of the free will He gave us, chooses not to.

God heard the cries of His people, the Israelites, for over four hundred years. When God set out to free His people, the hurdle He came up against was man's free will. First, Moses had to agree to take on the mission, which he ultimately agreed to with the help of Aaron. Then, Pharaoh became the obstacle. God had to get past Pharaoh's free will. It took some doing to break Pharaoh's spirit before he chose to release the Israelites.

On a smaller scale, how many of you have struggled with the free will of a teenager. As parents we may think we are in control until one day when our child begins to exercise his or her own free will. Their free will can be our biggest obstacle in our desire to protect and bless our children. Yet, it is our goal as parents to relinquish to our children their personal boundaries in the same way that God has relinquished our boundaries to us.

~~~~~~~~~~~~~~~~~~~~

How many of us have questioned why a loving God would allow so much suffering to go on in our world. From the very beginning, starting with Adam and Eve, God has allowed us our choices. And from the very beginning, we have corporately suffered for the choices mankind has made. Mankind is responsible for the atrocities of this world — not God. He allows it, as we so accusingly put it, because He will not rob us of the frighteningly powerful responsibility we have of owning our free will. Because of our free will, God teaches, admonishes, destroys, disciplines, and graciously gives us guidelines that we can choose to live by or not. God has turned people into pillars of salt, brought mighty armies to destroy nations, healed the sick, and blessed entire nations because of the belief of one man. At one point, God flooded the world saving only Noah and his family. God does respond to mankind's expression of free will — when He chooses and how He chooses. In the end, we are each left with a free will, which makes us responsible for our thoughts, feelings, beliefs, behaviors, choices, needs, and values.

If God were to strip us of our free will we would not have the capacity to love. In giving us a free will, God created us with the potential to love. It is what separates us from animals. We are not limited to living by what we call animal instinct. We live from our "free will." Love can only come from our personal boundaries. It is out of our thoughts, feelings, beliefs, behaviors, choices, needs, and values that love will find a way. God could not have programmed us to love because then it would not be love. If, when God created us, He programmed us to behave in loving ways, we would be nothing more than robots and our loving behaviors would mean nothing. Love can only come from a free will. Ultimately, in our relationship with God it becomes possible to love both God and man. That can be the beautiful outcome of our free will. We can choose to ask God to teach us to be more like Him. That will happen as we continue to know God, love God, and desire the things He desires.

How it must break God's heart to watch me make bad choices over and over again. Yet, in spite of the sorrow it might bring Him, He never robs me of my free will. I can believe Him or not believe
~~~~~~~~~~~~~~~~~~~~

Him, accept His instruction or reject it. I can spend time with Him or neglect Him. I can do good in relation to others or do harm to others. I freely choose every day of my life what I will do with my personal thoughts, feelings, beliefs, behaviors, choices, needs, and values. (We will build on this concept through the rest of Part Two.)

I Am Responsible For My Boundaries:

Once you become a Christian, the Holy Spirit is in you. He is there to teach you, to guide you, to comfort you, to counsel you, to empower you with love, to grow fruit in you that can only come from the Spirit of God. The fruit of love, joy, peace, and patience... He is in you and those things are now possible. What makes it possible? Two things — the Holy Spirit living *in* you and the Holy Spirit living *through* you.

We know that the Spirit of God lives *in* us. He is born in us when we accept Christ. So then why doesn't it just happen? Poof! Supernatural living!? It is because in order to live the supernatural life the Holy Spirit must also live *through* us. Therefore, it is very important that we learn about who the Holy Spirit is, and how He begins to live *through* us.

~~~~~~~~~~~~~~~~~~~~

> "*Now the Lord is the Spirit,* and where the Spirit of the Lord is, there is freedom. And we all, with unveiled face, beholding the glory of the Lord, are being changed into his likeness from one degree of glory to another; for this comes from *the Lord who is the Spirit*" (II Corinthians 3:17-18, italics added).
>
> "Jesus said to him, 'Have I been with you so long, and yet you do not know me, Philip? *He who has seen me has seen the Father;* how can you say, 'Show us the Father'? Do you not believe that I am in the Father and the Father in me?" (John 14:9-10a, italics added)

~~~~~~~~~~~~~~~~~~~~

Scripture tells us "The Lord is the Spirit." Jesus said, "He who has seen me has seen the Father." Jesus equates them one to another. Therefore, what is true of God is true of Jesus and what is true of Jesus will be true of the Holy Spirit. In light of that, let's ask ourselves again, did Jesus force Himself on you? No. And neither will the Holy Spirit. Even after He has entered in, after He has been born in you, He will wait for an invitation because you were created in the image of God. You have a free will as a Christian, to invite the Spirit of God to live through you, or to live life in your own strength. Becoming a Christian will not take away your free will. Therefore, you have the privilege of exercising your free will daily — constantly.

Some of you might hear this and think, "Good, I'm still the boss; I'm still in control, in the driver's seat." If you are inclined to think that way, it is because you have not yet come to fear your will in the way that I have come to fear mine. This is the scariest piece of information I am going to give you. You have a free will.

I have seen and experienced the ramifications of my free will. I have seen where it leads. I know what kind of mess I am capable of making. The thing I most fear is my free will. I do not trust myself with my free will. I do trust God's will for my life. God says, "I know the plans I have for you... plans to prosper you and not to harm you, plans to give you hope and a future" (Jeremiah 29:11 NIV). If you desire to live the life that God has planned for you to live, then you may ask Him to empower you to live that life.

You may choose to make this your prayer: "Spirit of God, live through me. Teach me to know and love your ways." This prayer is not a "once and for all time" prayer as was your invitation for Him to live in you. You may choose to give your will over to God every time it desires to have its own way. In the garden of Gethsemane Jesus yielded His will to His Father's when He said, "Not my will but thine be done."

We may daily invite the Spirit of God to live through us. As we grow to love His ways, we will begin to experience less struggle in giving up our own will, because we will begin to desire His. Learning to love His ways will come only as we learn to love Him. We grow to love Jesus as we spend time with Him. It is in His presence that we will fall in love with Him.

Study Questions

Chapter Eleven
Free To Ask

What is one of the things that God has given us that sets us apart from all other living creatures? ______________________________

Does God force you to obey His will? ____________________

Where your personal boundaries are concerned, you are responsible for your own...

______________, ______________, ______________,
______________, ______________, ______________,
and ______________.

In relation to adults, you are not responsible for anyone else's. (With the exception of adults having specials needs for which you are acting as caregiver.)
You are responsible __________ the people that your boundaries impact. You are not responsible __________ another (adult) persons boundaries.
Relationships get into trouble when one of two things happen. What are these two things?

1) ______________________________________
2) ______________________________________

In my counseling practice I have found that we all have a natural tendency to violate boundaries in one of these two ways. We will either be more apt to forfeit our boundaries to someone else, or we will have a tendency to want to control other's boundaries. Which of these two tendencies are you most likely to practice?________________

____

When have you experienced unhealthy control in a relationship?

____

____

When have you been the unhealthy controller? ________________

____

When have you forfeited a boundary in an unhealthy way?

____

____

How might you have responded differently? ________________

We have all been on both sides of forfeiture and control. Becoming aware of our tendencies allows us to approach God in truth. We can then ask Him to teach us how to love responsibly.

~~~~~~~~~~~~~~~~~~~~

In attempting to protect and bless us, what is God's greatest hurdle? ____

What can be the beautiful outcome of your free will? __________

____

In order for us to see the fruit of supernatural living in our lives, two things must become a reality in our lives. They are:

1) ____,

and

2) ____

What part do we play in experiencing God living through us?

____

Why must we ask God to live through us? ________________

____

What is the scariest piece of information given to you in this chapter? ____

Why is this so scary? ________________________________

____

How will we grow to love Jesus? ________________________
~~~~~~~~~~~~~~~~~~~~

How has the busyness of life impacted your relationship with Jesus? ______________________________

____

____

____

What are the distractions that keep you from nurturing your relationship with Him?

____

____

____

Prayer: Father, I am sobered by the fact that You lovingly give me over to myself. I realize I can choose to live in close fellowship with You or choose to ignore You. I want to know You more. I want You to be involved in every part of my life. As You respectfully wait for an invitation, teach me to ask more of You.

Chapter Twelve

Free To Know God

We are free to ask the Holy Spirit to be involved in our lives. We are free to ask Him to be our constant companion. What an amazing impact this can have on our lives. It puts us in a position to know God and His will for our lives.

> "Do not be conformed to this world but be transformed by the renewal of your mind, that you may prove what is the will of God..." (Romans 12:2).

Proving the will of God. That is quite a claim! Can you prove God's will? How many Christians desperately desire to know God's will for their life? They want to do His will; they are just not sure what His will is. There are so many questions; there is so much confusion. Always choices! People ask, "What is the will of God?" That is often the big question. But I ask you first, "What is the *mind* of God?" You cannot know His will without first knowing His mind.

"Let this mind be in you, which was also in Christ Jesus" (Philippians 2:5 KJV). We are to have the mind of Christ! In order to *have* the mind of Christ, we must *know* the mind of Christ. We can only know the mind of Christ by knowing Christ, personally and intimately.

Our hearts and minds are transformed inside of a relationship with Jesus Christ. There will be no transformation outside of that relationship. Now you might think, "I have a relationship with Christ, I gave my life to Him X-number of years ago and I've been involved in the church ever since." The fact that you received Christ as your Savior is wonderful. But it does not say anything about your relationship with Him today. Jesus wants an ongoing intimate relationship with you. That is where transformation will begin for each one of us. It is where it began with His disciples.

~~~~~~~~~~~~~~~~~~~~

> "And he went up into the hills, and called to him those whom he desired; and they came to him. And he appointed twelve, to be with him, and to be sent out to preach and have authority to cast out demons" (Mark 3:13-15).

~~~~~~~~~~~~~~~~~~~~

"And He appointed twelve, to be with Him...." Jesus wanted His disciples, first, before anything else, to simply "be with Him." Jesus says, "Come to me." The transformation occurred not in the going out and doing. My guess is that would have led to arrogance and pride in themselves. The transformation occurred in *being with Jesus*. They experienced from Jesus meekness and humility. That is where transformation will begin for each one of us. We need to spend time with Jesus, personally, all by ourselves. Not via somebody else. It is not enough for us to spend time with other Christians. We have the great privilege and opportunity to develop and nurture our own relationship with God. Become His best friend. Make yourself known to God, and He will make Himself known to you. "Draw near to God and He will draw near to you" (James 4:8).

~~~~~~~~~~~~~~~~~~~~

During my first marriage I was cut off from fellowship with other Christians. I did not attend church, Bible studies, or any other Christian functions. Christianity was a huge thorn in the relationship,
~~~~~~~~~~~~~~~~~~~~

so I did as little as possible to irritate that sore spot. My Christian life revolved around my Bible, my Lord, and me.

It was during those difficult years that I began to know Jesus Christ differently than I had ever known Him before. Why? I believe it is because He became my source. Not the church, not other Christians, not someone else's interpretation of spiritual things — nothing but Jesus. I learned how to *be with* Jesus, as opposed to *going to* Jesus.

Our society has developed this concept of *going to* God. We go to Him in prayer, perhaps in the morning, and in the evening, and possibly a couple of times throughout the day. But next time you go to Him, don't leave Him; take Him with you into every part of your day. Instead of going to Him anymore, simply turn to Him and talk to Him because you are already with Him. You do not have to "go" someplace if you are already there. Spend your entire day with Him, spend your week with Him, and spend your life with Him.

The apostle Paul had learned to be with Jesus. Paul's source was Jesus. Let's look at the life of Paul.

~~~~~~~~~~~~~~~~~~~~

> "For I would have you know, brethren, that the gospel which was preached by me is not man's gospel. For I did not receive it from man, nor was I taught it, but it came through a revelation of Jesus Christ.... But when he who had set me apart before I was born, and had called me through his grace, was pleased to reveal his Son to me, in order that I might preach him among the Gentiles, I did not confer with flesh and blood, nor did I go up to Jerusalem to those who were apostles before me, but I went away into Arabia; and again I returned to Damascus" (Galatians 1:11-12, 15-17).

~~~~~~~~~~~~~~~~~~~~

Paul heard from God. God spoke, Paul heard, and Paul went out on one of the most enormous missions in all of history without conferring with flesh and blood. He did not discuss it with anyone else. What Paul did amazes me. I can't go to a special event without conferring with friends about what to wear! Paul went out to preach to the Gentiles without conferring with flesh and blood. I'm glad he did, being the gentile that I am. I'm glad Paul thought it was enough to let God lead with or without mankind's approval. Paul spent a lot of time learning from the Lord, not from the disciples, not from other believers, just the Lord — one on one. There was no confusion. He knew God's will.

Paul had learned to listen to God. Paul was content to be alone with God. He removed himself from the distractions of the world, from swaying opinions and influences of other people, and he chose to listen only to the voice of God. This is an important example for us to follow. As Christians we simply have not learned to sit in silence in order to listen and learn from our Lord. We live in a noisy world, where words are thrown at us continually. We do not know what to do with silence. Life so preoccupies us with things other than our God that we do not know how to concentrate on Him. When given the opportunity to listen in silence and be with Him, we will habitually turn on the T.V., or the radio, or call someone on the phone.

We can learn from Paul and his desire to listen and talk with our Lord. As we sit in silence with Jesus we will begin to know Him as we have never known Him before. We will begin to recognize the whisper of His voice. The still small voice of Jesus will grow louder and clearer when it is surrounded by silence.

> "Ask, and it will be given you; seek, and you will find; knock, and it will be opened to you" (Luke 11:9).

When we seek to be with Jesus, we will find truth. He responds to our heart. When He sees the desire in our heart to know Him personally, He will reveal Himself to us. Then God will begin to unlock scripture, and the mysteries that have remained hidden will come alive. The Spirit of God will become our teacher. God desires for us to know Him. He desires to unlock the simple, profound truth that is safely kept for those of us who desire to know Him. And when He does unlock the truth to you, it will be for you alone. It will be for the sake of freedom — your freedom. The truth will set you free. You will not boast of your new-found understanding of scripture because it will not be revealed without your first finding your way to Jesus' feet. You will have first experienced the miracle of gentleness and lowliness of heart. The lowly have nothing to boast about. From the feet of Jesus you will go forward with a desire for truth. Ask and it will be given you. Ask to see and understand. Ask for the Spirit of God to reveal to you the heart and mind of God.

~~~~~~~~~~~~~~~~~~~~

> "For what person knows a man's thoughts except the spirit of the man which is in him?" (I Corinthians 2:11)

~~~~~~~~~~~~~~~~~~~~

Jesus calls us to be with Him, and as a result, we begin to know Jesus not only as Savior, but also as Lord. Our Lord will equip us to go out with confidence. The thing He equips us with is trust. The time that Paul spent alone with God was enough to send him out on the risky, unthinkable ministry of preaching to the Gentiles. Paul must have trusted God an awful lot. He knew God well enough, personally, to trust God's direction and leading. When Jesus said, "Go and preach to the Gentiles," Paul said, "Okay, I'll go." We are free to know God, and in knowing God we find ourselves free to obey.

Study Questions

Chapter Twelve
Free To Know God

What must we become familiar with before we can know the will of God?

____

In Mark 3:13-15, Jesus called some men to join Him up in the hills: "And he went up into the hills, and called to him those whom he desired; and they came to him. And he appointed twelve, to be with him, and to be sent out to preach and have authority to cast out demons" What two things were these men appointed to do?

1) ______________________________________
2) ______________________________________

Jesus is calling you and me to be with Him. Spending time with Jesus, getting to know His heart and mind is how we will come to know His will. The will of God in Mark 3:13-15 is so exciting because it points to a life that is less about vocation and more about how you approach your vocation, whatever it might be.

First, we can approach every part of our lives in the company of Jesus who desires to be with us. It is a message of love and belonging. He invites us to live in His presence. We can extend that message of love and belonging to others. We can love others with respect for their boundaries and a measure of grace that they will be drawn to. They will want to belong to our God.

Second, He protects us by giving us authority over the powers and principalities of this world. Those demons have one objective, and that is to take us as far away from the truth as they can. Their aim is to veer our attention from God and His truth to either Satan and his lies, or to ourselves and our hurts. The demons of this world are too many to name. We have all come up against them. It might have been a spirit of fear, criticism, bondage, hate, envy, lust, or oppression. The authority we have over these powers is the Spirit of God.

The Spirit of God lives in us, and by the authority of that Spirit we can speak to any form of evil that desires to come against us.

In Chapter three we began to look at how Satan takes the truth, wraps it with shame, and serves it up to us as a lie. We believe the lie because it looks so much like the truth.
How will the truth become clearer to us? ____________________

There are many things that prevent us from spending time with Jesus in order to listen and learn.
What are some common things that people tend to fill silence with?

____

____

What do you tend to fill silence with? ____________________

In practicing sitting alone with God, some people have expressed frustration with their inability to concentrate solely on Him. Their thoughts wander to whatever is going on at work or at home. It has been my experience that when my thoughts go in a specific direction, that is not my wandering away from God, instead it is God wanting to go there with me. He is very much interested in every part of our lives — work, home, and play. God wants to discuss and be a part of our entire lives.
Practice sitting in silence with God... (What things began to come to your mind? What did you find yourself wanting to talk to Him about? What did you find yourself motivated to do? Summarize what you and God discussed or did as a result of your first sitting with Him in silence.)

____

____

____

We will not always have the opportunity to spend quiet, peaceful time alone with God in the busyness of our lives. It is, therefore, important that we practice not only sitting in silence with God, but also doing what Brother Lawrence calls, "practicing the presence of God." In practicing His presence we can continue to talk to God throughout the day, wherever we are and in whatever we do. As we practice God's presence we learn that we are never out of His presence. We don't have to "go" to God in prayer, instead we can simply turn to Him constantly throughout the day. All of life becomes a prayer.

Paul was motivated to go out and preach to the gentiles after spending time alone with God.
When have you tackled a project or participated in a ministry that God motivated you to do? ______________________________

____

What was your experience in that ministry? ________________

____

Prayer: Father, it amazes me that not only do You want me to ask things of You, but that You, the creator of all things, out of respect for my "free will" or "boundaries," ask things of me. You ask! It amazes me even more that the first thing You ask of me is to simply be with You. You want to be with me. Father, sit with me. In the busyness of my life, I fail to just sit in Your presence. What a comfort it is to know that I don't need to approach You with well thought out words. I can approach You with no words at all. You are my God and I am Yours. Forgive me for all the neglect You have experienced from me. The people I love most are often the people I most neglect. Thank You that You are interested in every part of my world. When my thoughts wander, You are wandering there with me. When I go about the busyness of my day, You go with me. Thank you, Father... Let's go.

Chapter Thirteen

Free To Obey

To know God is to love Him. We do begin to love God as we get to know Him. It is how we fall in love with anyone, by spending time with them learning about who they are. When we share our heart and mind with someone, we develop an emotional intimacy with them. As Christians our emotional connectedness with Jesus will determine how we respond to the word "obedience." Most of us will have one of three responses to the word obey. 1. A subtle, even unconscious feeling of resentment for being "told" what to do. 2. A performance based response that operates either out of duty or out of efforts to avoid shame. 3. A desire to obey. This chapter will look not only at our response to obedience, but also at our God who, initially, desires only that we obey.

Our Response To Obedience:

1. Some of us have turned the word obedience into a negative word. We associate it with subordination or a giving up of control. Obedience is relegated to kids and dogs, not adults. The word obey has become a word that implies an action is being taken that is contrary to the wishes of the one taking action. We only obey because we have to. Where God is concerned, we do not have to. God will not take from you your free will. He is a respecter of boundaries. Earlier I mentioned the scariest piece of information that I would

give you, and here we are faced with it once again — you have a free will. Part of what makes it so scary is our response to obedience. We think it is about God wanting to control us.

Bless and Protect:

Obedience is not about God controlling us. It is an attempt by God to bless and protect us. God does not want to control us. If He did want to control us He would not have given us a free will. The fact that He uses the word obey is evidence that He does not want control. The very word obey implies that we have a choice. We can choose to obey or not obey. Obedience does not rob us of our free will; it confirms that we have a free will. He asks us to obey.

He does want to influence us. That is why He gives us instruction. We have given a name to the ten things He graciously wrote on stone and gave to Moses. We call them the Ten Commandments. Scripture is full of advice and admonition on how we should approach life.

There are some of us who while we may still cringe at the word obey, have experienced enough of God personally to trust Him. We may choose to obey God, not necessarily because we desire to, but because we trust that He has our best interests at heart. We may not yet see the importance or relevance of our obedience. God allows us, therefore, to simply obey because we trust and not because we understand. Thank goodness for that. God desires that we receive His direction, even before we are able to understand why He directs as He does. While we are still spiritually blind to many things, He desires that we trust.

A young child trusts his parent blindly at first because the child believes that the parent has his best interests at heart. The relationship between a parent and a young child is founded on authority. The child initially can only be told what to do because he is not yet capable of understanding the reasons behind the guidance. The child is taught not to play in the street or put an object in a light socket. It would not be wise for the parent to wait until the child was capable of understanding why he shouldn't play in the street, because to wait would put the child in danger. Therefore, it is enough that the parent says "no" to the street and calls it "danger." "Danger" is the first and simplest concept to be taught the child. Some day in the future the child will understand the specific danger related to streets and light sockets. So too, will we someday understand more clearly the dangers that surround our lives and the reasons why God desires to protect us from those dangers. Obedience is not about what we are doing for God. It is about what God is doing for us.

Our God so desires to protect and bless us that, initially, He does not even care whether we desire to be obedient or if we understand why we ought to be obedient. He only asks that we obey. He does not care about the motive of our heart because He knows it is impossible for our motives to be pure, they cannot initially be pure because we have not yet been made pure. When we first accepted Jesus as our Savior, He did not say to us, "You have to be sorry for your sins, or don't bother coming to me." To be truly sorry for our sins we would have to love God, and love is the very thing that has to be developed in us — it is not there yet.[8] We did not love God enough to be truly sorry, but He saved us all the same, in spite of the fact that we did not love Him with all our heart, with all our soul, with all our strength, and with all our might.

2. Some of us will obey God out of a performance-based mindset. We may not have experienced yet, the freedom that the Holy Spirit works in us as He teaches us to separate the lies we live by from the truth. We are still controlled by shame. We will, therefore, perform for God, or obey, in order to avoid the shame that we would be flooded with if we did not obey. When this happens we can hardly even call it obedience. It is an attempt to receive God's acceptance, approval, affirmation, and admiration based on works. This performance-based merit is false; God does not accept us based on what we do. If that is what we believe, we have not yet found the freedom of God's unconditional, graceful love.

<u>"If You Love Me":</u>

I have grown increasingly aware of the reality that love for God is often a matter of lip service. You may tell Him you love Him, but do you? Do you love Him with all your heart, with all your mind, with all your strength, and with all your soul? Or is love for God something that you only desire to have with all your heart, mind, strength and soul. Perhaps you have not yet learned to love Him. It is quite impossible to fully love God when love is the very thing that needs to be developed in us. Until the Spirit of God teaches us to love, we cannot love as God would have us love.

~~~~~~~~~~~~~~~~~~~~

> "If you love me, you will obey my commandments" (John 14:15 GNB).

~~~~~~~~~~~~~~~~~~~~

A person could easily read this verse and set out to prove their love for God by trying hard to obey His every command. Many Christians do just that; they attempt to live by the letter of the law. We may read this verse and immediately think that God is asking us to perform. Thus, we enter into a life of performance for God. We think that way because, often, we live that way. All of life is about performing, even our spiritual life.

I believe these words of Jesus say far more than, "try your hardest to obey me." I believe they are informing us of the secret to the abundant life. They are telling us that the key to obedient living is loving God. "[When] you love me, you will obey."

I do not believe Jesus is saying, "Prove your love to me by doing what I tell you to do." Many insecure men and women approach love this way. They will say, "If you love me you will do this or that for me." We think that love is proven by whether we remember our anniversaries, or by buying nice things for each other. We may say, "If you loved me you would stay home with me and not go out bowling with the guys." Many people attach external behaviors to the proof of love.

I do not believe Jesus attaches anything external to love. He knows that love, although it may be expressed externally, can exist only within us. It is a matter of the heart. If and when we truly love God, then we will obey His commands. Then it will happen. Obedience will be the outcome of love.

3. True obedience to God comes when we at last have fallen in love with the one who meets us in our sinful state and says, "You are mine — I love you." We begin to return a love that comes from our heart, a love that says, "Yes, I love you too." It is out of our love for God that we will eventually find ourselves with a desire to obey. A desire to obey is supernatural and it begins to make possible a type of obedience that is supernatural. Obedience becomes possible not only from our natural condition which allows us to choose to obey whether we like it or not, but also from a supernatural perspective. Heartfelt obedience comes as God changes or transforms our minds, allowing us to see things from His perspective. God's commands are quite impossible for us to do in and of ourselves. God asks us to love in ways that are unreasonable....

> "But I say to you that hear, Love your enemies, do good to those who hate you, bless those who curse you, pray for those who abuse you. To him who strikes you on the cheek, offer the other also; and from him who takes away your cloak do not with-hold your coat as well. Give to every one who begs from you; and of him who takes away your goods do not ask them again. And as you wish that men would do to you. Do so to them."
>
> "If you love those who love you, what credit is that to you: for even sinners love those who love them. And if you do good to those who do good to you, what credit is that to you; for even sinners do the same. And if you lend to those from whom you hope to receive, what credit is that to you: Even sinners lend to sinners, to receive as much again. But love your enemies, and do good, and lend, expecting nothing in return; and your reward will be great, and you will be sons of the Most High; for he is kind to the ungrateful and the selfish. Be merciful, even as your Father is merciful" (Luke 6:27-36).

God asks us to love in outrageous ways. Ultimately, we are able to obey not because we are able to love our enemy, but because He is able. He does it in us, because in us is where He lives. Obedience is possible. Invite Him to obey through you. Ask Jesus for the power to obey. In doing so, you are not asking Him for the energy to do all the tasks to which you have committed yourself. In asking for the power to obey, you are asking for the power to love. Obedience is the key to loving your enemy. Obedience is an opportunity not a duty.

Obedience:

As our minds are transformed inside of our relationship with Jesus, we will become more and more able to discern what is the will of God. As we learn His will we have more opportunities to obey. As we obey we understand more of the mind of Christ because obedience leads to further understanding. God does not ask us to understand and then obey! He asks us to obey and later understand!

Obedience is a demonstration of belief, and as we will learn in the next chapter, believing leads to seeing. Our obedience will lead to seeing, not just with our eyes, but with our hearts and minds as well. We will begin to understand God's purposes and His ways as we obey. The Holy Spirit will begin to unlock the mysteries within Scripture and reveal spiritual truths that we would have remained blind to apart from obedience.

Whatever you know to be God's will, do it. Having done His will, you will not ask, "Why did I do that?" You will instead understand more fully why God asked it of you. As Christians we do not hesitate to pray for wisdom and knowledge. We are all too eager to pray for discernment, but seldom, if ever, do we ask God for the strength to obey. Make this your prayer: "Father, give me the strength to obey."

Study Questions

Chapter Thirteen
Free to Obey

How do we develop an emotional intimacy with someone?

____

____

At what time in your life did you feel the most emotionally connected to God? ______________________________________

____

How emotionally connected do you feel to him today? _________

Life's demands often pull us away from our priorities and cause us to lose our emotional closeness to God and the people we love most. When we take time to share our heart and mind with the people we love it will change the way we respond to them in our everyday lives.

This chapter suggests that the emotional intimacy we have with God will influence the way we respond to the word obey.

I. Many of us have turned the word obedience into a negative word. We think it's about God wanting to _______ _______________ us. In truth, God asks us to obey so that He can ____________________ and ___________ ________________ us.

What did God give us that is evidence of the fact that we are indeed in control of our lives? ___________________

We may choose to obey God, not because we ________ ____________ to, but because we _________________ that He has our best interests at heart.

II. Some of us will obey out of a ___________________- _______________ mind set.

We obey in order to avoid feelings of ___________ _________. We are actually attempting to win God's ______________, ________________, _______________, and _______________. (The A words.)

God does not love or accept us based on what we do. He loves us because we are His children.

God does not say to us, "Prove your love to me by doing what I tell you to do." He understands that when we love Him, then we will obey out of a desire to obey.

While love may be expressed _____________, it is a matter of the ______________________________

III. As we grow to love God, we begin to desire obedience. We begin to develop a heart like God's. We begin to desire what He desires and want what He wants. We will begin to see ourselves loving others in a way that is supernatural. Heartfelt obedience comes as God ___ _______________ our minds allowing us to see things from His perspective. When we ask God for the power to obey we are asking Him for the power to _________ ________. Obedience is an __________________ not a __________________. It is an opportunity not only to receive God's blessing and protection, but also an opportunity to understand more clearly the heart and mind of God.

How do you most often respond to the word "obey"? __________

1) With resentment for being "told" what to do.
2) A response associated with feelings of duty. (Shame-based)
3) With a sincere desire to obey.

Think of a time when you have found yourself "doing" or "obeying" out of duty or guilt. ________________________________

____

What motivated you to say "yes" to something that, in your heart, you believed a "no" would have been a better answer?

____

____

____

Often when we take on a project that we are not excited about, we are preventing God from being able to bless someone who would love to be given that responsibility. There are also times when our inability to say "no" keeps programs or activities alive that should die out. Some projects are driven by man and not by God. We can let those projects end so that people can put their energy into doing the things that God would truly motivate them to do. We can say "no" to what we do not feel led to do, so that we can say "yes" to the projects we would love to be a part of.

Prayer: Father – Your love for me is something I cannot begin to understand. I do not know how to love You the way that You love me. I have not learned how to love well yet, but I know You will help me to learn. Thank You for blessing and protecting me even when I do not recognize the many ways You do that. You ask me to love my enemy, and yet You know what is in my heart. Give me the strength to obey. Gently lead me to the place where I will desire to obey.

Chapter Fourteen

Free to See

Blind trust does not come easily or naturally to us. We have learned over the years to turn over our "childlike" faith and replace it with "adult like" skepticism. The faith of most adults is no longer faith. It has been poisoned with the logic of the world that says, "Seeing is believing." The faith of the world says, "I'll believe it when I see it!" But we will learn from Scripture that there is no faith in that kind of logic, because as faith would have it, *believing leads to seeing.*

I am afraid logic will not help to explain this idea, yet it is completely consistent with every spiritual truth that God has ever taught me. In every area that I have sought God's teaching, I have found it to be completely contrary to what the world teaches.
God's teaching:

- You must die to live.
- When you are weak, then you are strong.
- When you are poor, then you are rich.
- You must give to get.
- Love your enemy.

Where is the worldly logic in any of that? Now here we are with another truth that flies in the face of logic. The truth that believing leads to seeing.

I'll See it When I Believe it!:

~~~~~~~~~~~~~~~~~~~~

> "Jesus said to her, 'I am the resurrection and the life, he who believes in me, though he die, yet shall he live, and whoever lives and believes in me shall never die. Do you believe this?' She said to him, 'Yes Lord; I believe that you are the Christ, the Son of God, he who is coming into the world."... "Jesus said, 'Take away the stone.' Martha, the sister of the dead man, said to him, 'Lord, by this time there will be an odor, for he has been dead four days.' Jesus said to her, 'Did I not tell you that if you would *believe* you would *see* the glory of God?'" (John 11:25-27, 39-40, italics added)

~~~~~~~~~~~~~~~~~~~~

"Did I not tell you that if you would believe you would see the glory of God?" Believing leads to seeing. They obeyed Jesus and they rolled away the stone. They watched as Lazarus, the dead man, came out of the tomb.

~~~~~~~~~~~~~~~~~~~~

> "Then came one of the rulers of the synagogue. Jairus by name; and seeing [Jesus], he fell at his feet, and besought him, saying, 'My little daughter is at the point of death. Come and lay your hands on her, so that she may be made well, and live.' And [Jesus] went with him.".... "While [Jesus] was still speaking, there came from the ruler's house some who said, 'Your daughter is dead. Why trouble the Teacher any further?' But ignoring what they said, Jesus said to the ruler of the synagogue, 'Do not fear, only believe'" (Mark 5:22-24,35-36).

~~~~~~~~~~~~~~~~~~~~

"Do not fear, only believe." What did his *believing* lead to? It led to *seeing*. Seeing the glory of the Lord as his daughter was raised from the dead. In both instances believing required something. It required obedience. An opportunity to obey presented itself, and their belief in God empowered them to obey. Their belief had doubt, but even still they obeyed. Can you imagine God saying to you, "Dig up the grave and let's open the casket." That is essentially what He said to Martha. Lazarus had been dead four days and was in his tomb!

Jairus' obedience seems much easier; all he had to do was ask. For Jairus, however, asking was not a small thing. He was a religious ruler and the religious rulers had some very strong opinions about Jesus. Jairus exposed himself as a believer in Christ. Asking is a form of obedience. Scripture reminds us that we do not have because we do not ask. "Ask and it shall be given to you." This is not a "name it and claim it" kind of asking. Asking is a boundary issue. Asking is respectful in that it understands that a "Yes" or a "No" can come from the asking. Asking does not demand our way nor does it forfeit our desire. Ask and hope, believing God will hear and respond in love. We do not know how He will respond because we do not see and understand the way He does.

~~~~~~~~~~~~~~~~~~~~

> "There was a rich man, who was clothed in purple and fine linen and who feasted sumptuously every day. And at his gate lay a poor man named Lazarus, full of sores, who desired to be fed with what fell from the rich man's table; moreover the dogs came and licked his sores. The poor man died and was carried by the angels to Abraham's bosom. The rich man also died and was buried; and in Hades, being in torment, he lifted up his eyes, and saw Abraham far off and Lazarus in his bosom. And he called out, 'Father Abraham, have mercy upon me, and send Lazarus to dip the end of his finger in water and cool my tongue; for I am in anguish in this flame.' But Abraham said, 'Son, remember that you in your
~~~~~~~~~~~~~~~~~~~~

> lifetime received your good things, and Lazarus in like manner evil things; but now he is comforted here, and you are in anguish. And besides all this, between us and you a great chasm has been fixed, in order that those who would pass from here to you may not be able, and none may cross from there to us.' And he said, 'Then I beg you, father, to send him to my father's house, for I have five brothers, so that he may warn them, lest they also come into this place of torment.' But Abraham said, 'They have Moses and the prophets; let them hear them.' And he said, 'No, father Abraham; but if some one goes to them from the dead, they will repent.' He said to him, 'If they do not hear Moses and the prophets, neither will they be convinced if some one should rise from the dead'" (Luke 16:19-31).

~~~~~~~~~~~~~~~~~~~~

"Neither will they be convinced if some one should rise from the dead." If they were to see someone rise from the dead, still they would not believe, because seeing does not lead to believing. Believing leads to seeing. Jesus rose from the dead and many refuse to believe in Him. Jesus is the one in whom we put our faith. Faith requires belief. Let's look at the example of Abraham.

~~~~~~~~~~~~~~~~~~~~

> "Thus Abraham 'believed God, and it was reckoned to him as righteousness.' So you see that it is men of faith who are the sons of Abraham. And the scripture, foreseeing that God would justify the Gentiles by faith, preached the gospel beforehand to Abraham saying, 'In you shall all the nations be blessed.' So then, those who are men of faith are blessed with Abraham who had faith" (Galatians 3:6-9).

~~~~~~~~~~~~~~~~~~~~
~~~~~~~~~~~~~~~~~~~~

Abraham believed God, and it was reckoned to him as righteousness. The righteous shall live by faith. Faith enables us to believe, and believing leads to seeing. Imagine the impact obedience had on Martha and Jairus. Whatever measure of faith they had prior to their acts of obedience, no doubt it grew enormously by the end of the day. Any "adult-like" skepticism they had in the morning had turned into a "child-like" faith by evening.

Obedience then, opens our eyes to see God more clearly, and in seeing God more clearly we will trust Him more. Ironically, it is a return to blind faith that opens our eyes. A child-like faith belongs to the meek and lowly. Self-importance continues to loosen its grip as we are transformed. Grace toward others becomes more of an option as we grow in our understanding of God's grace toward us.

God's Grace – God's Love:

I learned about love when I experienced God's grace. I did not experience my own ability to love; I experienced God's ability to love me. I found a love that made me unafraid of mankind, a love that gives me a whole new footing in life. It is a love that will prevent me from being knocked down or blown away by every critical or unkind remark that comes my way. It is a love that does not weigh my good deeds against my bad deeds hoping to keep the scale tipped in the right direction. Love is not about performing, or God would certainly not be able to love me. Love is about grace. If I am to love others, it is going to have to be about grace. Grace will allow me to love you and grace will be the only way you will be able to love me.

If I cannot approach you with grace, I will not be able to approach you with an unconditional love. I would be a fool to approach you at all. You do, after all, have a great capacity to hurt me, as I do you. This world is now and will always be a risky place. If my focus remains on what you are capable of doing to me, then I might as well go find a cave and hide out until Jesus comes. After all, you might not like me. You might have a different opinion than I do about something I hold very dear to my heart. I may not approve of your choices. Our differences may be large or they may be seemingly insignificant. For most of us, it is a "one size fits all" reaction to anything that might take a bite out of our self-esteem.

Some of you may be thinking, "I could care less what anybody thinks of me. Whether you agree with me or like me is of no concern to me." This is eventually a great place to arrive at, if when we give up our self-protection it allows us to approach those people with love. Too often, however, our hardened, uncaring attitude towards people who do not like us or do not agree with us is a defense mechanism that allows us to not have to relate to them at all. It is just another form of self-protection. In such a case, the purpose of our hardened attitude is not so that we can love the other person; instead, it allows us to not even care about the other person. This lack of caring is not the end result we are looking for.

Born to Destroy:

The field of psychology is making great strides in using research to explore relationships. I am very grateful for the efforts of John Gottman and his team who are coming up with real answers to why relationships succeed, and why relationships fail. In assessing the health of relationships, Gottman looks for what he calls the Four Horseman of the Apocalypse.[9] These are four things that have proven to destroy relationships.

The Four Horseman of the Apocalypse:

1) Criticism
2) Defensiveness
3) Contempt
4) Stonewalling

Criticism feels personal because it is personal. It is directed at you.

"You never care about what I think."

"You always have to have the last word."

Criticism is about your failures and shortcomings. A perfectly natural response to criticism is to defend yourself. In **defending** yourself you attempt to turn the failures off of yourself and onto the accuser.

"I'm not the problem, you are."

"You don't listen."

Back and forth, round and round. Most attempts to repair the downward spiral are met with some form of **contempt**... sarcasm, cynicism, eye rolling, mockery, name-calling, sneering, or hostile humor.[10]

"Ya, like that's really gonna help."

"Oh that's just brilliant."

You can almost see those eyes rolling, can't you? These forms of contempt portray a level of disgust that does far more to damage than reconcile.

Stonewalling seems the best choice when the criticism, contempt, and defensiveness become too overwhelming. Stonewalling is silence. It is giving the cold shoulder. It gives us a temporary break when we feel too flooded with negative emotions to stay in the relationship. In truth, stonewalling sends a message of disrespect as it demonstrates a lack of value and validation toward the other person and their concerns.

Gottman's Four Horsemen of the Apocalypse do a marvelous job of portraying what I see as being mankind's sinful nature. The term, sinful nature, is something we Christians are all taught we have. We are born with it. Well, there it is. We are born knowing how to be critical, contemptuous, defensive, and exclusive. Nobody had to teach us how to do any of that. It is as easy as rolling off a log. Our natural tendencies come from our self-centered perspective. We can expect contemptuous, defensive, and critical words from people. It is what we all know. It is how we all attempt to protect ourselves. The problem is, it doesn't work. It serves only to wound others and ourselves.

The face value of our words often have little to do with what is truly in our hearts. Too often, our words do less to heal and more to destroy. God can see that our words are often nothing more than a veneer, covering up our hurting, uncertain hearts. The way God sees things and the way we see things are very different. God sees into the other person's heart. We are busy looking out for our own hearts.

See as God Sees:

Let's go back to the outer courtyard where Peter denied knowing Jesus three times. In Part One of this book we looked at Peter's perspective of failure and brokenness. Jesus was in that outer courtyard with Peter. What was Jesus' perspective?

If you or I had been in Jesus' place, how might we have responded if we knew that one of our best friends denied knowing us, not once but three times. How crushing it would be; how lonely and rejected we would feel. Our focus might not be on Peter's redemption, it more than likely would be on our feelings of abandonment. Our natural tendencies would not allow us to focus outside of ourselves. Jesus saw things very differently that morning. He was not focusing on Himself; He was still loving Peter even as He was on His way to the cross. Jesus turned and looked at Peter when the cock crowed that morning. Jesus was looking outside of Himself. He was not looking at Peter with criticism and condemnation. He was not feeling attacked or crushed. While Peter's internalized focus could see only failure and shame, Jesus' externalized focus was able to see victory and redemption. Jesus knew that at last Peter would begin to understand the truth about God's love. Jesus sees in truth. Until we come to the end of ourselves we cannot see outside of ourselves.

The ultimate example of Christ's freedom is demonstrated after His experience on the cross. When Jesus returned from the grave He never made mention of the atrocities He endured. He did not need a psychotherapist in order to work through issues of unforgiveness, or abandonment. There was no Post Traumatic Stress to deal with. No, Jesus hit the ground with both feet running. He was not focused on Himself; He was focused on the object of His desire — the bride of Christ. His church is what He was focused on. He was driven by love.

The supernatural life we begin to experience as we invite Christ to live through us is our only hope of breaking free from the self-protective bondage that comes naturally to us. As the Holy Spirit begins to open our eyes in a way that allows us to look outside of ourselves, life becomes full of purpose and meaning.

But It's Not Working!:

There are many of us who do pray these words, "Live through me, Lord," and still we often struggle with a sense of frustration, uncertainty, or woundedness. Perhaps we need to look more closely at what we are asking for. Are we truly asking for all that goes along with God living through us? Or are we using those words with the intent that God will then give us the will power to do what we want to accomplish? Does "live through me" simply mean give me the strength to get through this long day that I have filled with my agenda? Does it mean give me the will-power to tolerate this insufferable person I must spend time with today? Sometimes the reason we find so much of what we do insufferable is because it may have little to do with God's agenda, and He is trying to stir us to move in a new direction. He is trying to get us to see things differently.

Perhaps you feel confident that you are doing exactly what God has laid on your heart to do, and still you are feeling burdened. Sometimes we find our situation insufferable because we have not yet learned to see or hear things in truth, as God sees and hears. When we ask God for things in prayer, He hears not only what is spoken from our lips, but what is spoken from our hearts as well. The truth that is in our hearts is often very different from the words that come out of our mouths. I believe that God responds to our heart first, not our words.

Jesus responded to Peter's denial not based on Peter's words, but based on what He saw in Peter's heart. What happened in both Jesus and Peter's heart was supernatural. Rather than Jesus feeling abandoned, rejected, and unloved, He was filled with compassion for Peter. Peter could have responded with any of the four horsemen we learned about earlier: 1) He could have been critical of Jesus for not using His heavenly authority to crush injustice, or 2) he could have defended himself with the fact that he had followed Jesus farther than any of the other disciples, or 3) he might have mustered up some contemptuous thoughts about what a fine mess Jesus has created for all of the disciples, or 4) Peter could have simply stonewalled Jesus at that point and said, "I'm out of here." Instead he saw the truth about himself and his inability to love as Jesus loves.

It became a turning point for Peter. In order for Peter to become the rock upon which Christ builds His church, Peter is going to have to know what to do with criticism, rejection, and abandonment. Peter is going to have to be able to look beyond himself.

Free to See:

~~~~~~~~~~~~~~~~~~~~

"And they went into Capernaum; and straightway on the Sabbath day he entered into the synagogue and taught. And they were astonished at his doctrine: for he taught them as one that had authority, and not as the scribes. And there was in their synagogue a man with an unclean spirit; and he cried out, saying, 'Let us alone; what have we to do with Thee, Thou Jesus of Nazareth? Art Thou come to destroy us? I know Thee who Thou art, the Holy One of God.' And Jesus rebuked him, saying, 'Hold thy peace, and come out of him.' And when the unclean spirit had torn him, and cried with a loud voice, he came out of him" (Mark 1:21-26 KJV).

"They came to the other side of the sea, to the country of the Gerasenes. And when he had come out of the boat, there met him out of the tombs a man with an unclean spirit, who lived among the tombs; and no one could bind him any more, even with a chain; for he had often been bound with fetters and chains, but the chains he wrenched apart, and the fetters he broke in pieces; and no one had the strength to subdue him. Night and day among the tombs and on the mountains he was always crying out, and bruising himself with stones. And when he saw Jesus from afar, he ran and worshiped him; and crying out with a loud voice, he said, 'What have you to do with me, Jesus, Son of the most High God? I adjure you by God, do not torment me.' For he had said to him, 'Come out of the man,
~~~~~~~~~~~~~~~~~~~~

> you unclean spirit!' And Jesus asked him, 'What is your name?' He replied, 'My name is Legion; for we are many.' And he begged him eagerly not to send them out of the country" (Mark 5:1-10).

~~~~~~~~~~~~~~~~~~~~

Here are two examples of Jesus responding to what He knows is in the heart of a man and not to the words that come out of the man's mouth. The man essentially cries out, "Leave me alone, I want nothing to do with you." Most of us would not have to be asked twice. But Jesus hears something that goes beyond the words. He sees in truth what the situation is and responds according to that truth. The story of the demoniac is so impressive in that while the man is speaking words that indicate he wants nothing to do with Jesus, he is simultaneously taking a posture of worship, pleading with Jesus to hear not what he is saying, but rather to see what he is needing. Jesus responds to the man's need. Jesus is able to hear and see the truth that transcends our words and actions.

It is not just the negative Jesus is able to see through. He is able to see through our polish as well. The false piety and spiritual veneer that many of us put on when we leave home is not what Jesus will respond to. We see this many times over when Jesus deals with the Pharisees. In chapter one we read about the Pharisee who had Jesus to dinner. Remember the sinner who so unconventionally made her way to Jesus' feet, weeping and wiping His feet with her tears. Jesus responds not to the polished, proper behavior of the Pharisee. No, Jesus responds to what is in the heart of the man:

~~~~~~~~~~~~~~~~~~~~

> "Now when the Pharisee who had invited him saw it, he said to himself, 'If this man were a prophet, he would have known who and what sort of woman this is who is touching him, for she is a sinner.' And Jesus answering said to him, 'Simon, I have something to say to you.' And he answered, 'What is it, Teacher?' 'A certain creditor had two debtors; one owed five hundred denarii, and the other fifty. When

> they could not pay, he forgave them both. Now which of them will love him more?' Simon answered, 'The one, I suppose, to whom he forgave more.' And he said to him, 'You have judged rightly.' Then turning toward the woman he said to Simon, 'Do you see this woman? I entered your house, you gave me no water for my feet, but she has wet my feet with her tears and wiped them with her hair. You gave me no kiss, but from the time I came in she has not ceased to kiss my feet. You did not anoint my head with oil, but she has anointed my feet with ointment. Therefore I tell you, her sins, which are many, are forgiven…'" (Luke 7:39-47).

~~~~~~~~~~~~~~~~~~~~

When we ask God to live through us we are asking for the power of truth to have its way in us. We are asking to see things in truth as they really are. It begins by God helping us to see ourselves in truth, and then it goes beyond that into our seeing others in truth as well. We are asking God to empower us to see into the hearts of the people we deal with. We are asking Him for ears that hear beyond the words they speak. We are asking for the truth about what we are faced with throughout the day. We begin to look at people in truth with the heart of God and find ourselves full of compassion and grace. Our understanding goes beyond our self-centered ability to understand. It is out of God's Spirit of Truth that we are then motivated to take action. We begin to *do* things out of the very real phenomenon of God living through us.
~~~~~~~~~~~~~~~~~~~~

Study Questions

Chapter Fourteen
Free to See

Many of us watch our "childlike" faith grow into ____________.

Unfortunately, we develop the logic of the world which says, "Seeing is ____________________."

This chapter points out another truth that flies in the face of worldly logic. The truth that believing leads to ____________________

Faith enables us to believe, and believing leads to seeing. Ironically, it is a return to blind faith that opens our eyes to see more of God's truth.

The "sinful nature" we are born with sets us up to be more mindful of ourselves and less mindful of others. It is our self-protective nature that makes it very difficult to approach others with love and grace. John Gottman looks for what he calls the Four Horseman of the Apocalypse in assessing the health of a relationship. The Four Horsemen of the Apocalypse are:

1) ____________________
2) ____________________
3) ____________________
4) ____________________

Write about a time when you felt criticized. ________________

____

A natural response to criticism is defensiveness. Did you defend yourself to the person who criticized you? (Either verbally or silently in your heart.) Did you defend yourself to others?

____

____

____

This pattern of "criticize – defend" exists in most relationships because it comes very naturally to us. Feelings of contempt are a natural by-product. Contempt may seem like too strong a word until we learn that the number one form of contempt is sarcasm. Sarcasm permeates our society. We have actually attached a value to sarcasm as being funny or witty. In truth, sarcasm allows us to say the opposite of the truth.

List a few ways in which you have used sarcasm.

1) ______________________________
2) ______________________________
3) ______________________________

In each case can you see that the opposite of the truth was spoken? If we spoke from sincerity and not from sarcasm what would those statements look like?

1) ______________________________
2) ______________________________
3) ______________________________

The fourth horseman, ____________________, allows us some emotional distancing from an uncomfortable situation. In so doing, we isolate and detach ourselves from those we care about.

Relating to each other outside of the four horsemen does not come naturally to us. It requires us to relate from a supernatural perspective. It requires us to approach life from a position of transformation.

We look again at Peter in order to see how his transformation took shape in the outer court when Jesus turned and looked at him. Peter, instead of becoming critical, defensive, or contemptuous, was able to at last agree with Jesus about his failures and shortcomings. The last thing any of us want is to be seen as a failure or as being weak. That is why criticism is so hard for us to take. Agreeing with someone who is attacking our performance falls way outside of our self-protective ways. And yet, agreement with someone, or the ability to see from their perspective is often exactly what is necessary in order for us to see things in truth as they really are.

Looking back at the time you were criticized was there any piece of the criticism that may have been valid? If so, what might it have been? ____________________

____

Think of a time when you were able to agree with someone about his or her concern. What was the end result of that encounter?

____

____

Jesus was criticized by the religious leaders of His day, and yet He never defended Himself to the people around Him. He never spoke sarcastically. He spoke the truth directly to the leaders when they addressed Him, but He never sought them out in order to set them straight about who He was. Jesus was not focused on Himself; He was focused on the object of His desire. What is the object of His desire? ____________________

Because we are the object of His desire, Jesus has the supernatural ability to see beyond what we say. He sees, instead, what is in our hearts.

In response to the demoniac Jesus did not feel rejection, instead He heard a cry from the heart of the man that said, "Love me in spite of my hurtful accusations." We have all been hurled insults, whether from an insensitive friend, or a rebellious child. It is a powerful thing when we are able to love someone well in spite of their words.

Can you think of two different times when you were wounded by words and your response was different each time? Once when you retreated, hurt by their words, and went into a self-protective position of defending and criticizing. And once, when you held your position, listened earnestly to what was being said, and responded in a sincere way to the heart of the individual.

1) ____________________

____

____

2)____

____

____

Prayer: Father, in the midst of a negative confrontation I often want to either fight or take flight. I either defend myself and accuse the other, or remove myself from that person all-together. I need help in finding validity to what they are saying. I need help in seeing what is in their hearts and how their hurts motivate them to hurt me. I am too protective of my own heart to see into the heart of another. Father, give me eyes to see into the wounded hearts of others. Give me ears to hear their secret cries for help.

Chapter Fifteen

Free to Fight

We are born with a desire to fight. Our natural tendency is to fight in order to protect ourselves. We fight for our safety, our rights, for justice, for our reputation. We often fight to do what is considered right. Naturally, we like to put ourselves in the best possible light and we fight to make the most of ourselves. As Christians, this natural tendency often expresses itself in a desire to be used by God. It is a noble desire. I do not believe, however, that it is always a pure desire. I do not think in fighting to be used by God, we are fighting the right fight.

In our relationship with Christ we learn that whether or not we are used by God becomes irrelevant. Far too much emphasis is placed on this concept. It is unfortunate when we see our elderly feeling empty and void of any value simply because they can no longer be "used." God does not call us to be used.

C.W. Tozer expresses my heart in his book, *Keys to The Deeper Life*: "We must reckon ourselves dead to gain and glory and allow ourselves to become inextricably involved with the cross of Christ and the high honor of God. Then our prayers will be something like this: O God, let thy glory be revealed once more to men: through me if it please Thee, or without me or apart from me, it matters not. Restore Thy church to the place of moral beauty that becomes her as the Bride of Christ: through me or apart from me; only let this prayer be answered. O God, honor whom thou wilt. Let me be used or overlooked or ignored or forgotten."[11]

God does not call us to be used; He calls us to something far better, and higher, and purer. He calls us to a life of faith.

~~~~~~~~~~~~~~~~~~~~

> "Fight the good fight of faith; take hold of the eternal life to which you were called" (1 Timothy 6:12 NAS).

~~~~~~~~~~~~~~~~~~~~

We are called to battle! We are to fight the good fight, the fight of faith. We cannot fight the right fight without faith in God. We can put faith in ourselves or in others, but that will not be the right fight. We can put our hope into the here and now, and do all we can to build ourselves up in this life. God, however, asks us to put our hope in the eternal, not in the here and now. He asks us to "Take hold of the eternal life to which you were called" (1 Timothy 6:12 NAS).

The fight of faith became an option for us when we took our very first step of faith by inviting God to make His home in us. It took a certain measure of faith to believe that Jesus is who He says He is, and accept His gift of salvation. That, however, is only the beginning of the workings of faith in our lives.

Faith is the necessary ingredient for which to do battle. The measure of faith we take into battle will undoubtedly affect the outcome. Faith, fortunately, is something that grows. Compared to a mustard seed in scripture, we learn that though it may start small it has the capacity to outgrow itself many times over again. In Matthew17: 20-21 we learn that if we have faith the size of a mustard seed we can move mountains. Wow! God does not want to send us into battle unarmed. Faith is powerful stuff. A mustard seed is a very small thing and yet just that much faith can move a mountain. I cannot help but ask myself, "How often do I find myself with less faith than could fit into a mustard seed?"

If faith is our protection in battle, our shield against the enemy, it makes sense that we would want as much faith as possible. Growing faith is a good idea. The place where faith grows is in the fertile presence of God. That is where we fall in love with God. That is where faith is multiplied. As we experience the newness of ourselves — meekness, humility, love, joy, peace, etc, — we experience freedom. Freedom is the most powerful faith builder. Putting faith in the one who sets us free from our self-centered bondage becomes easy. Having come face to face with the love of Christ, I am prepared to put my faith in Him. Think of the supernatural claims that are made in scripture regarding the outcome of my transforming faith in Christ. It is hard to imagine that it could actually lead me to a place where I would love my enemy, or do good to those who persecute me, or produce a joy and peace in my life that would not be contingent on my circumstances. Most importantly, I might finally experience what it is to love the Lord my God with all my heart, mind, strength, and soul. What a place that will be.

<u>The Battle:</u>

There is a battle to be fought. We need to know *how* and *where* that battle is to be fought.

~~~~~~~~~~~~~~~~~~~~

> "Take every thought captive to obey Christ" (2 Corinthians 10:5b).

~~~~~~~~~~~~~~~~~~~~

The implications in this verse are enormous. The fact that there is a captive indicates that there must indeed be a battle. The fact that the captive is a thought indicates that the battle must be in the mind. It is no wonder the part of us that needs transformation is the mind — the mind is where the battle takes place. "Be transformed by the renewal of your mind" (Romans 12:2).

Not only does the battle take place in the mind, the battle is for the mind. The mind is our control center. Whoever or whatever controls our mind, controls us. Faith enables us to enter the dangerous battlefield of our mind. Our thought life will be assaulted with heavy arsenal. The arsenal the enemy will use against us in battle are lies. Lies are the secret weapons of the enemy. He wants us to believe what is not true. Satan knows that the truth will set us free. Therefore, he wants to keep us from believing the truth. He wants to make us prisoners of war; he wants us in bondage.

The deceiver would love for us to believe all the lies he feeds into our minds. We touched on one of the ways he does that in Part I of this book. He takes the truth, wraps it up with shame, and serves it up to us as a lie. We believe the lie because it looks so much like the truth. As each thought enters our mind we need to take hold of it (capture it), look at it in truth, call it what it is, and give it an appropriate response. Either keep it as truth, or discard it as a lie. Do not let the lies even settle in your mind. Keep them moving.... in one ear, and out the other. SWISH!

The Power of Lies:

I had the great privilege of meeting with a young man who was in search of an intimate and real relationship with Jesus Christ. I will call him Neil. In spite of the wonderful Christian upbringing he had and the solid teaching he had been raised with, he found his life was lacking in what the church calls "the abundant life." He was not experiencing freedom in Christ. In truth, he was experiencing what felt like a life of bondage. The Christian life as he understood it was simply a long list of things to do that he believed should be a reality in his life, but were not. The harder he would try to do what he believed a Christian should do, the heavier the burden of life would weigh on him.

When asked to write out his definition of what it means to be a servant of Christ, he wrote down the following.

A Servant of Christ

- Selfless.
- Always praying and thinking of others.
- Doing things for others through service and ministry.
- Talking with others and being genuinely interested in the life of the one your talking to.
- Supporting others.

- Sharing Christ with those who don't know Him.
- Not being easily annoyed with people.
- Stepping beyond my fears to help someone.
- Being ready to meet other people's needs.
- Sacrifice.

It is a beautiful list. You can imagine Neil's confusion when I looked at that list and called it a lie.

Neil is a very talented and gifted young man. He loves music and spends a great deal of time composing and practicing. He is also a very gifted writer and hopes to one day make a living from either of these two talents. When he is not working hard at the two things he wants to pursue as a career, he is off playing tennis, which is his third passion in life.

Neil had been counseled by numerous well meaning people that perhaps it was not right for him to be putting all his energy into listening to music, writing stories, and playing tennis, at the expense of getting out there and living "the Christian life." He was made to believe that in order to be a true servant of Christ, he needed to put all his energy into getting out there and doing the list of things that a servant does. Let's look again at what Satan does to us when feeding us lies. He takes the truth, wraps it up with shame and serves it up to us as a lie. Neil's list looks a lot like the truth. Neil's list, however, was wrapped in shame. For Neil, the lie felt like this: "Shame on you, Neil, for enjoying something that is of no value to God. Shame on you for wasting your time and putting your energy into things that are not spiritual."

Neil thought perhaps he could spiritualize his life a little bit by at least not enjoying the life he led. So music, writing, and tennis all became a heavy burden. "I'll do it, but I won't enjoy it," he thought. "Instead, I'll feel guilty, not only for wasting my time on these things, but also for being so good at it."

The message of shame was so overwhelming that the truth became totally obscured. If I were to write a definition of what I believe it means for Neil to be a servant, it would look something like this:

Neil,
A servant of Christ

Enjoy music, write, and play tennis with gratitude to God, and in fellowship with God.

When Neil is finally free to live, and love, the life that God has given him, then he will experience a life with Christ that will include the beautiful things that Neil had on his list. Until that day comes, Neil's list will remain a burden to him. Why? There is a battle going on in Neil's mind. It is a battle between truth and lies. The lie Neil is holding onto is that his value comes from his performance. The burden he feels comes from trying to accept a belief that feels conditional. Only an unconditional belief about God's love will set us free, because it is the unconditional nature of God's love that is truthful. The truth sets us free. Neil's idea of servanthood cannot bring freedom because it is not truthful. It is built on a lie of condition. Neil's idea of servanthood cannot be true when it is wrapped up with shame.

Neil's idea of servanthood will never be lived out in the flesh. It will never be a life that you can set out to obtain on your own. The life of servanthood is an outcome of your personal relationship with Jesus Christ. Whatever life God gives you here on earth is to be loved, enjoyed, appreciated, and lived to the fullest, *as* you enjoy living in constant fellowship with Him.

I would be in a good deal of trouble if being a servant of Christ meant being a successful musician, an excellent tennis player, and a proficient writer. For me it means something entirely different. It means being a wife, mother, daughter, sister, and friend who spends most of her energy playing. I plan lots of treasure hunts and tea parties. I am in love with the life God has given me. There have been some who would like to redefine for me what it means to be a servant. But I have learned that there is no way in which I can better serve God than to love Him, enjoy Him, and live to the fullest the life He has given me. It is a life of being loved, and of loving the people that fill my world. When we see in truth the simplicity of God's love for us, then we will be free to respond in healthy ways to the many people He puts in our path. Our ability to enter into this life with God can easily be thwarted, however, when we are not able to separate the lies from the truth.

Neil's perspective of the Christian life was based on performance and not love. I'm glad Neil sensed that something was very wrong with his view of Christianity and his view of God. He was longing for an unconditional love, and his understanding of God placed a heavy burden of condition on how he approached life.

How it must break God's heart when He sees us working so hard to earn His favor. It robs Him of the closeness He desires to have with each one of us. We are robbed of this closeness when we believe the lie, once again, that God's love for us is conditional; the lie that we must perform a certain way in order to win His love.

Imagine a young child, age 1 to 5, trying hard every day to earn the love of their mother or father. What if the toddler made desperate attempts daily to earn acceptance, approval, affirmation, and admiration, believing that a failure to perform could separate him from his mother or father's love. Imagine the child worrying constantly about what would please his parents, perhaps asking, "What can I do to win your love today; what can I do to earn your favor?" As a mother, the very idea breaks my heart. I wanted nothing more than for my children to fall into my arms with the complete certainty that they were each the object of a depth of love that could not even be defined. At night during "tuck-in time" we would attempt to define our love for each other but could not. I'm sure many of you have had similar dialogues with your young children….

"Good night, I love you."

"Good night, I love you more. I love you this much." (With arms outstretched as far as they will go.)

"I love you around the whole world."

"I love you googolplex."

"I love you infinity."

There was never a definition that felt big enough.

I enjoyed watching my children play, laugh, sing, and learn. If I had thought for a moment that they were worried about performing in order to win my acceptance it would have broken my heart. And it still would break my heart today. There is nothing to earn. I love them infinity. (Unless there is a bigger word.)

Part of loving our children requires discipline. We discipline in order to bring about obedience. Why? For two reasons: 1) Protection, and 2) Blessing. We want them to learn adaptive behaviors that will work well for them in life. We teach them to say "please" and "thank you." We teach them to share their toys. We want to build in our children character qualities such as: generosity, humility, a good sense of humor, sincerity, compassion, and a strong work ethic.

We attempt to guide them in ways that will instill all these good traits in their lives, not because we want them to perform for us, but because these things will pave the way for them to go out and lead fulfilling lives. We want them to know what qualities to look for in a future spouse. We want them to have a work ethic and character qualities that will enable them to get a job and keep a job. We want to teach life skills. None of what we teach as a parent should have a string attached to the love we have for our children. It is a tragedy when any one of us begins to believe the lie that says there is a string attached to love. It is a tragedy when we begin to view ourselves as being unworthy or unlovable. As we grow out of childhood we begin to believe lies about what makes us good or worthy or valuable.

There is no such thing as a perfect parent, child, or friend. We all fall short in our attempts to love perfectly. There is a perfect God - who is our perfect Father. Regardless of our earthly experience, we have a God who loves us with no condition on that love. It is safe to put our faith in God. Faith in God is essential to our growing up and experiencing successful, fulfilling lives. God delights in our well-being.

<u>Faith Our Fuel:</u>

> "Without faith it is impossible to please [God]" (Hebrews 11:6).

We might read this and think that faith, in and of itself, is what is pleasing to God. While I'm sure our faith in God does please Him, this verse is saying that it is not faith itself that is pleasing, but rather it is faith that puts us in the position of being able to please Him. "Without faith it is impossible to please God" (Hebrews 11:6). It is impossible because without faith we will not believe what He teaches. If we do not believe, we will not obey.

~~~~~~~~~~~~~~~~~~~~

"Take every thought captive to obey Christ" (II Corinthians 10:5b).

~~~~~~~~~~~~~~~~~~~~

Here we have stumbled again on to the very thing that pleases God — obedience. Without faith it is impossible to please God, because without faith we will not obey. The fight of faith is fought in our minds as we take every thought captive. We take every thought captive in order for the outcome of our faith to be pleasing to God — "Obey Christ." Why is obedience so pleasing to God? For two reasons, 1) Protection, and 2) Blessing.

First, He asks us to obey for our protection. Obeying God protects our relationships, our health, and our hearts from the fallout of unforgiveness. While obedience may be the weapon that protects us, faith is the fuel that gives power to obedience. Without faith we would not put our trust in God in order to obey.

Second, obedience is the avenue by which God will be able to bless us beyond measure. It is for us and our well being that He asks us to obey, it is not for His own sense of power. God does not have an ego that we need to feed in order for Him to feel all-powerful. God is all-powerful with or without our obedience. God is omnipotent, omniscient, and omnipresent. God is free, He is love, and He is just. God IS already! That's why He can say, "I AM." God asks us to obey because He has a plan for our lives that is contingent on our having faith to obey.

~~~~~~~~~~~~~~~~~~~~

> "'For I know the plans I have for you,' declares the Lord, 'plans to prosper you and not to harm you, plans to give you hope and a future'" (Jeremiah 29:11 NIV).

~~~~~~~~~~~~~~~~~~~~

Wow! Now that is a plan that I can come along side. I want to join God in His plans.

Set the Mind:

In order for His plan to come about we must take every thought captive, hold it up to the light of truth, and thus discern how to respond to that thought. Do we keep it as truth, or discard it as a lie? Because the battle revolves around truth, it is very important that we know the truth. It is very important that we know Jesus, because He is the truth. The world, the flesh, and the devil are going to throw all kinds of unhealthy, untrue thoughts our way. We need to know what to do with each thought.

~~~~~~~~~~~~~~~~~~~~

> "To set the mind on the flesh is death, but to set the mind on the Spirit is life and peace" (Romans 8:6).

~~~~~~~~~~~~~~~~~~~~

The battle is fought in the mind, at the thought level. If we allow it to go beyond the thought level, we will lose the battle. Not the war, but surely the battle. When we take it beyond the thought level we turn it over to the flesh. That's when we go from thinking to doing. Once we have given in to temptation, we lose the strength necessary to resist it. Strength comes prior to temptation, at the thought level. Once our flesh is involved, we have gone too far. We did not take that thought captive. That is why Jesus taught us to pray, "Lead us not into temptation." Once we are into it we have no strength.

Too often we set our limits *within* the boundaries of temptation. Our thought is, "I will enter into temptation, but I will only go so far." "I will taste the fruit, I just won't eat the whole thing." We make well-intentioned boundaries for ourselves that we hope we will have the will-power to keep. Regretfully, we will find ourselves staring at that boundary with the strength of our flesh, because that is what we are left with once we enter into temptation.

It is all too easy to give in to temptation. It is easy for us to sacrifice God's will for our own will, because we have not yet learned the truth about our own will. We have not learned how costly it can be. We have not learned how unkind, how untrustworthy, how dangerous it can be. We do not fear our will — in most cases we desire our will. There is little hope of our obeying God's will when we so strongly desire to have our own will satisfied. In every instance God will leave us with the choice to choose our ways over His. But His love is such that should we decide to choose His will, He provides His very own Spirit to empower us with the faith to obey. He will instill in us a measure of faith that says, " I will believe in God - I will believe that He desires only good things for me - I will trust Him." It becomes a fight of faith.

Study Questions

Chapter Fifteen
Free to Fight

There is a battle to be fought. Where does the battle take place?

____

What does God arm us with to go into battle? _______________

____

How much faith do we need to move a mountain? ____________

____

In the fight of faith, we are to take captives. What is it we are to take captive? ____

What does being a servant of Christ mean to you? ___________

____

____

Neil's perspective of servanthood was based on performance, not love.
Have you ever felt that a condition was being placed on you that was somehow attached to the love you would receive? ______________ _____. Having performed the necessary tasks, did you feel loved? _ _________________. Having failed to perform the necessary tasks, did you feel loved? _______________________________________

We have a God who loves us unconditionally.

The fight of faith allows us to take every thought captive in order for the outcome of our faith to be pleasing to God. What is the outcome that God is hoping to see? ____
What two things come out of our obedience to God?

1) ______________________________, and
2) ______________________________.

What are some ways that God protects us when we obey Him?

___

___

How are we blessed when we obey? ___

___

___

God asks us to obey because He has a plan for our lives that is contingent on our having faith to obey:
"'For I know the plans I have for you,' declares the Lord, 'plans to prosper you and not to harm you, plans to give you hope and a future....'" (Jeremiah 29:11 NIV)

Without faith we would not put our trust in God in order to obey. Taking every thought captive allows us to fight the battle in the way it must be fought, and in the place it must be fought. The way we fight is by separating lies from truth; the place we fight is in our thought life. If we allow the battle to go from thinking to doing then we are at risk of losing the battle. Not the war, but surely the battle. That is when we enter into temptation. Then we are faced with the real dilemma of wanting what we want, rather than wanting what God wants. Our "free will" will always be given the opportunity to have its way.

Can you think of a time in your life when God's instruction was overshadowed by a strong desire to have what you want? ___

___

___

Perhaps in hindsight we can look back and find it easier to believe in God's direction as being *for* us and not *against* us.

Are there any areas in your life that you still struggle with in attempting to obey God? (Loving your neighbor as yourself, coveting what is not yours, addictions, etc.) ___

As God continues to reveal truth to us about ourselves and others, it becomes possible to fight the battle of faith at the thought level. We will no longer be held captive to the lies we have held onto. We will begin to see in truth and respond in truth. The truth will set us free to engage in the fight of faith.

Prayer: Father, more often than not, I find myself defending lies and not truth. I place a standard on others and myself that is not motivated from freedom. Instead, it only puts others into the same bondage that I have lived under. It is the bondage to perform. How can I possibly extend grace to others when I have yet to accept it from You. Thank You that You have opened my eyes to see the truth about Your love for me. Thank You that I can now go from working hard in the flesh, to serving You freely in the Spirit of Truth.

Chapter Sixteen

Free To Love

The purest form of love I have experienced apart from God's love was when my children were born. It was different from the love I experienced with spouse, parents, siblings, or friends. The thing that made it different was the complete lack of expectation. The love I felt for the infant was given with absolutely no expectation on the baby to perform a certain way, think a certain way, or even to love me in return. I was free to love without attaching anything to the gift of my love. I loved that baby for free, simply because it was mine. Not only was the love given freely to the child, it was also given with no expectation placed on me. There was no worry of living up to the child's expectations, because the baby was not capable of having an expectation. I could not fail. I could not say the wrong thing, or do the wrong thing. Forgiveness was entirely unnecessary because there was no concept of falling short.

It sounds beautiful, doesn't it? The only thing that could be more beautiful than the safe, pure love that exists between a parent and a newborn child is the love of God. Imagine that same freedom of love exchanged between myself and another when both are fully aware of my shortcomings and failures. A relationship in which receiving love is not contingent on what I do or what I say. I am loved by God, not because I deserve it, or have earned it, but because I am His. The powerful unconditional love of God is directed at you because you are His.

When we see in truth the reality of God's love for us, it then becomes possible to extend that same love towards others. The powerful, unconditional love of God becomes ours — ours to live in, and ours to give. We become free to love. This ability to love others can only happen when we no longer fear the truth about ourselves. God's love for me allowed me to look honestly at myself. Knowing that nothing could separate me from His love allowed me to look truthfully at my shortcomings and imperfections.

~~~~~~~~~~~~~~~~~~~~

In my counseling practice I am often confronted with people who are unable to look honestly at their failures and shortcomings. Their self-esteem can't afford to. A low self-esteem causes us to hunger for acceptance, approval, admiration, and affirmation (The "A words"). We hope that the "A words" will build up our esteem. Looking at our failures and shortcomings will only lower our esteem. Therefore, we develop a fear of failure and enter into a life of performance. Our hope is that if we perform well enough we might earn the acceptance and approval of others. Our performance is a form of control. It controls whether or not our self-esteem gets fed its much-desired affirmation.

Our performance may take one of two forms: 1) We may learn to forfeit our list of boundaries (thoughts, feelings, beliefs, behaviors, choices, needs, and values) in hopes of arriving at the "A words." It may seem easier and safer to forfeit our belief for someone else's belief, our choice for theirs. We will simply do what the other person wants done, becoming little more than an extension of someone else.[12] 2) We may force our way onto someone else, thereby sending a self-serving message to ourselves that says, "I'm right, I'm needed, I'm indispensable." We might rescue someone from the natural consequences of an irresponsible behavior by simply not allowing them that irresponsible behavior. We will demand that things be done "my" way, which of course is the "right" way. We insist on preventing other people's mistakes.[13] We hope that such superior qualities will make us worthy of those "A words." The problem is they do not. The truth is that forfeiture of boundaries, or
~~~~~~~~~~~~~~~~~~~~

control of others' boundaries, will have the exact opposite effect. It will lead to deep resentment and disrespect on both sides. We find ourselves caught in a pattern of living that will only serve to wound us further.

We are wounded by others when we do not receive from them the acceptance and approval that we long for. We compound the wounds as we interpret from our own thought life a sense of inadequacy, lack of value, and unworthiness. We hold on to a belief that says, "If I just work harder, do the right things, or say the right words, then I will be worthy of acceptance and approval." While we hold onto the hope of earning their love, we may simultaneously fault those who are depriving us of those "A words" as being insensitive, uncaring, and heartless for deliberately hurting us.

Our compulsive need for approval often plays itself out in seemingly loving, caring, and giving ways. Many Christians hide behind a life of what looks likes sacrifice, all the while longing to be set free from a life of working hard in the flesh. We crave the nurturing that comes when we are praised for our performance. In truth, such nurturing is false and empty. It cannot fill the emptiness we feel inside. Such approval is conditional. Our hard work often serves only one purpose, which is to alleviate for a moment the consequences of our not performing. To not perform or do what is expected of us leaves us open to enormous risk — the risk of experiencing rejection, abandonment, or possibly just being thought less of. We cannot handle someone thinking less of us. That would be counter to our ultimate goal — the "A words."

These futile attempts to feel good about ourselves will never work. We were not designed to be dependent on man and his opinion of us. We were designed to be dependent on God. If, in fact, we have come to see the truth about ourselves and our sinful condition, then performing for God becomes ridiculous. God most certainly does love and accept us for free; His love is unconditional.

When we get caught in the web of needing to perform in order to feel good about ourselves it becomes impossible for us to have a healthy response to an unhealthy behavior. A healthy response might require us to say "no" to an unreasonable request. A request becomes unreasonable, not necessarily because of the nature of the request, but because of how it may impact our lives. In deciding if a request is unreasonable we might first ask ourselves, "Will this task take me away from a family that has already forgotten what it's like to have me around? Does this request line up with what I am truly motivated to do, or am I being motivated by a false sense of duty or shame?" If saying "no" to an unreasonable request puts us at risk of not receiving the "A words," then we might not say "no." We might say, "yes" and make way for resentment and bitterness to build. We cannot love others responsibly or well when we fear possible rejection or disapproval. It is important that we learn to love our "no" as well as our "yes."[13]

Perfect Love Casts Out Fear:

God's perfect love casts out the fear we cling to in loving others. The vulnerability we fear in holding to our own boundary is laid to rest. We are at last free to live by our own convictions when we are no longer enslaved by the opinions of others. When God's unconditional love fills up our nurturing need, then we are no longer in need of the "A words" to fill our nurturing deficit. We can love others from an overflow of God's love, rather than needing others to love us in hopes of their filling our love deficit.

Perhaps you have, in the past, focused so intently on responding to other's thoughts, opinions, and expectations that you do not even know what your boundaries are anymore.[14] You are safe with God to explore who you are. What are your beliefs? What is your opinion? What choice is true to who you are? While you reestablish your boundaries you can rest in the knowledge that God knows and loves you while you do not even know what you think, feel, or prefer. He loves you because you are His. Your relationship with God is the only perfectly nurturing relationship you will ever have on this side of heaven. He nurtures you with His kind of love; a love that bears the fruit of love, joy, peace, patience, kindness, goodness, gentleness, faithfulness, and self control.

What an amazing God we have. He is a God who first crushes us with the truth of our sinfulness, only so that He can then bless and nurture us with the outrageous power of His love. He knows what we long for and He knows there is only one path that will lead us to our heart's desire. He offers us a love that is not based on condition. It will never be earned or won. It is ours in spite of who we are — it is ours because of who we are. We are His children, and He simply loves us.

Loving You?:

In chapter fourteen we learned from Gottman about four things that destroy relationships: criticism, defensiveness, stonewalling, and contempt. When we are at last operating out of an overflow of God's nurturing, unconditional love, then we can trade in our destructive patterns of relating to others for healing patterns. We can lay down our defensive, self-protective ways. We replace the four destructive messages for three healing messages. They are: 1) Value, 2) Validation, and 3) Respect.

1) A message of value at home can be, "I care about you more than anything in the world," or "I value your opinions and I want to share in your dreams and goals." At work it might be, "I really value your input and welcome your ideas." When we say to a co-worker, "I will give that some serious consideration," it lets them know they have been heard. A message of value leads to a feeling of safety within the relationship. It is the kind of safety that offers respect for another person's point of view. When we do not feel valued, we cease to offer up an opinion because we develop the attitude that our ideas do not matter anyway, so why bother.

2) Validation takes us a step farther into the healing process. We validate people when we not only value what they have to say, but we find validity in it. When we are able to agree even in part, with what someone is trying to communicate, we assure him or her they are being heard and understood. Too often, if someone has a differing opinion from our own, we immediately shift into our defensive mode. Rather than look for possible merit in the other person's opinions, we begin formulating our thoughts on how to prove or defend our own opinions.

Looking for opportunities to validate is easy. Any time you feel criticized, stop before you speak, and in your mind turn that criticism, into a valid concern or complaint. Listen to what that person is trying to say to you. Try to understand the impact their concern has on *them*. Look outside of yourself and any feelings you may be experiencing that are causing your defensive strategies to kick in. If the words you are hearing feel caustic or critical, look beyond the words that are being spoken and instead, look into the heart of this person. Their heart is looking for something. It is looking to be valued and validated. It wants to be heard and understood.

In healthy, satisfying relationships both people are able to be positively influenced by each other. If one or both individuals are unable to be influenced, the relationship is on a destructive course. How easy is it for you to say things like:

"That's a good idea."

"I need help."

"You're right."

"I don't know."

"I'm sorry."

"I'm not sure."

"What do you think about this?"

"Thanks, that's good advice."

These types of comments are evidence of a willingness to be influenced. They point to an ability to be part of a shared relationship. These individuals are not looking to be controlled, nor do they want to control.

3) If we are not able to give a message of value and validation to others, we will not be able to offer respect. Respect is all about boundaries. Respect first allows us the privilege of determining what we think and believe, and then it allows us to extend that privilege to others. Self-respect is often the missing component that causes respect for others to become twisted or distorted. It becomes forfeiture or control, and not respect. Until we know and respect our own boundaries, we cannot respect another's boundaries. Instead, we will simply find ourselves either living by another's boundary or being offended by another's boundary and wanting control.

In the movie, *Run Away Bride*, Julia Roberts plays the part of a young woman who goes from relationship to relationship simply becoming whatever her current boyfriend wants her to become. At the end of the movie she is faced with a simple question that requires her to make a choice, "How do you like your eggs?" Up until that point in her life, the simple choice of egg preference had been determined by someone else. She realized she did not truly know how she liked her eggs. It may seem like such a simple boundary issue that for many it becomes unimportant. It is these simple boundary issues, however, that are the easiest place to start. There are many people that draw a blank when faced with looking at their boundaries. They have had so little practice at having their own opinions and choosing their own preferences that they simply don't know what they prefer.

The freedom to differ, however, begins with self-respect, and with that, the understanding that allowing yourself a personal belief or a preference is not selfish as many unfortunately feel. It is simply taking ownership of the life God intended for you to own. You can then respectfully allow others to own their lives. Honoring each other's differences becomes an option when being different is not a threatening thing. If I prefer scrambled eggs and my husband prefers fried eggs, I can now choose, not to forfeit my boundary, but to give the gift of fried eggs to my husband when he knows my preference would have been scrambled.

Giving to others from a secure set of boundaries becomes a life of submitting one to another. It is done from a position of strength not weakness. It is offered from an overflow of love not from a deficit of love. Rather than needing to be filled, I can operate from the fullness I find in owning and tending the precious "free will" that God has given me. A "God like" love can only come from our free will. That is why God gave us a free will. We must know our boundaries so that we can love from our boundaries.

Inside the safety of respectful relationships there is opportunity for ideas to be shared and people to be influenced in healthy ways. The ability to translate a criticism into an honest complaint allows us to respond to the need of the individual rather than react out of self-protection. It allows us to love well.

Study Questions

Chapter Sixteen
Free to Love

What are the four "A words" that we all hunger for?

1) ____________________________
2) ____________________________
3) ____________________________
4) ____________________________

These are the things that keep our self-esteem afloat. We sometimes fear our failures, weaknesses, and shortcomings, believing they will somehow strip of us of the "A words" we have worked so hard to achieve.

Our desire for acceptance and approval is often what launches us into a performance-based lifestyle. Our performance may take on one of two forms. Briefly describe these two forms of self-protection:

1)____
____
____

2)____
____
____

The problem with both of these efforts to win approval is that they do not work. Instead, they will lead to deep ____________________ and ______________________ on both sides.

We are wounded by others when we do not receive from them the approval and acceptance we long for. One way we protect ourselves from woundedness is to work hard at being good. Our compulsive need for approval often plays itself out in seemingly caring and giving ways. Have you ever agreed to take on a job or ministry for the wrong reasons? ______________________________________

If so, what? ____

What motivated you to say "yes" to that request? ______________

Are there certain people in your life that you feel it is safe to say "no" to, and certain people that you find it harder to say "no" to? If so, who are they? ______________________________________

____

When others do not respect our "no," it makes it harder for us to believe in our "no" as being a positive and healthy response. We need to learn to love our "no" as much as our "yes."

Can you think of a time when you successfully said "no" when it was hard for you to do so?__________________________________

____

____

In this chapter we learn that we can replace our destructive patterns of relating to others with healing patterns.
The destructive messages include: (The Four Horsemen of the Apocalypse)

1) ____________________
2) ____________________
3) ____________________
4) ____________________

The Healing messages are about:

1) ____________________
2) ____________________
3) ____________________

We send a message of value when we take the time to listen to another person's perspective on an issue that is important to them. Healing increases when we not only listen, but also validate what they are saying. The respect we demonstrate by valuing and validating another person's point of view is essential in building healthy relationships. (As we begin to recognize the individuals who ask us to perform for the wrong reasons, it is important to note that it is not our job to get them to love our "no." That person may never change.

We can still learn to give them a message of value and validation, as we respectfully say "no.")

Inside the safety of respectful relationships there is an opportunity for ideas to be shared and people to be influenced in healthy ways.

The ability to translate a ____________________ into a valid ______________ or ____________________ allows us to respond to the emotional need of the individual rather than react out of self-protection.

Prayer: Father, teach me to lay down the destructive messages of criticism, defensiveness, contempt, and stonewalling. Teach me instead to give messages of value, validation, and respect. Teach me when to say, "Yes," and when to say "No." Teach me when to speak and when to be silent. Teach me how to love others with the strength of love that You demonstrate toward me.

Chapter Seventeen

Free to Serve

"We serve not under the old written code but in the new life of the spirit" (Romans 7:6b).

The old written code led us to death. Jesus resurrected us to a new life in the Spirit. This new life frees us from a life of works, in order that we be free to serve. You might ask, "What's the difference?" Works! Service! It all sounds the same. It hardly seems possible that freedom could look like service. The world would teach you the opposite. The world would equate freedom with being served or, at the very least, freedom would be viewed as being able to do "what I want." The world doesn't understand service. Many of us are unable to separate working hard in the flesh and serving in the Spirit of God. The first is far from freeing. The second can only be done in freedom. I believe it is impossible to serve apart from freedom. Why? Because service is a supernatural thing. It is a supernatural life. Jesus called himself a servant. His life was supernatural. Service is done in the supernatural power of God's love.

~~~~~~~~~~~~~~~~~~~~

> "Rise and stand upon your feet; for I have appeared to you for this purpose, to appoint you to serve and bear witness to the things in which you have seen me and to those in which I will appear to you, delivering you from the people and from the Gentiles – to whom I send you to open their eyes, that they may turn from darkness to light and from the power of Satan to God, that they may receive forgiveness of sins and a place among those who are sanctified by faith in me" (Acts 26:16-18).
>
> "Whoever would be great among you must be your servant, and whoever would be first among you must be your slave; even as the son of man came not to be served but to serve" (Matthew 20:26-28a).

~~~~~~~~~~~~~~~~~~~~

This is the supernatural life that God offers us. A life of Service! It is service done, not simply in the name of God, but in the love of God. God loves you with a perfect love – a perfect, unconditional, free love. His perfect love sets us free to love others with His love, unconditional and free. We can freely love the one who is not free to love us. We can love the one who expects us to perform, without feeling compelled to perform. We can unconditionally love the one who puts conditions on us because we are free from the bondage of sin and shame.

Changing the World Around Me:

Many of us as Christians desire to do great things for God. We set out with noble intentions to make a difference in the world around us. We want to go out and save the world. (If not the world, at least our corner of the world.) Unfortunately, we learn quickly that we are not able to carry out our desires. We find ourselves helpless in our ability to change people's hearts.

One of the beautiful outcomes of the transformed life in the Spirit is that we are at last equipped to make a difference. In fact, it becomes impossible for us not to make a difference. With the Holy Spirit living through us, it will be impossible for our lives not to have an impact on people.

King David tells us of God's miraculous outcome when we are made new by the Spirit of God.

~~~~~~~~~~~~~~~~~~~~

> "Create in me a clean heart O God, and renew a right spirit within me. Cast me not away from thy presence and take not thy Holy Spirit from me. Restore unto me the joy of thy salvation, and uphold me with thy free spirit. Then will I teach transgressors thy ways, and sinners shall be converted unto thee" (Psalm 51:10-13 KJV).

~~~~~~~~~~~~~~~~~~~~

Not until we have been made new by the Holy Spirit will we see the fruit that comes from a new creation. King David's prayer must become our prayer too: "Create in me a clean heart O God. Uphold me with your free spirit and keep my heart clean. *Then* I will see sinners converted unto thee." Then it will happen. It is impossible for it not to happen. It is what happens when our lives are given over completely to the will and workings of the Spirit of God. The Spirit of God changes hearts. We don't. The Spirit of God draws us to God. It is His miracle. It is His doing. When the Spirit of God has at last been given the daily opportunity to live through you, your life will bear witness to the power and strength and peace of God.

Too many Christians go through life apart from the freedom they could be experiencing in Christ. They are saved, yes, but not free. Seek freedom. Grace is prepared to set you free. It desires to set you free. If only we would live with the one who alone can make us free.

What Makes Work Good?!

The life of service becomes supernatural in its outcome.... "Sinners shall be converted unto thee" (Psalm 51:13). Others will be drawn to the strength of God that they experience through you. This strength will look like confidence, peace, humility, and conviction. It will offer grace and not condemnation. It will be inviting. Its draw will stem more from who you are than what you do. We will all be doing a great deal. The difference comes in what motivates the doing and what the Spirit of God will reap from the doing. All of a sudden, we are free to do what scripture calls "good works."

~~~~~~~~~~~~~~~~~~~~

> "For by grace you have been saved through faith; and this is not your own doing, it is the gift of God — not because of works, lest any man should boast. For we are his workmanship, created in Christ Jesus for good works, which God prepared beforehand, that we should walk in them" (Ephesians 2:8-10).

~~~~~~~~~~~~~~~~~~~~

Here we learn that out of our supernatural life of service comes good works. The Spirit of God sets us free to give up a life of "works" and enter into a life of "good works." The irony of this shift is that the task we commit ourselves to may not change at all, because it is not about the task. Whether we are a butcher, a baker, a doctor, or a homemaker, the outcome of God's transforming Spirit will be that you will cause others to be drawn to God. Good works are not about what we do, it is about how we love. Whether we are 19 or 90, others will be drawn to the love of God and sinners will be converted unto Him. You won't need to practice or perform this thing called evangelism in the power of your own strength. It will be a supernatural outcome of God's grace being expressed through you. Evangelism cannot be defined in form. It can only be defined in function. Its function is to lead people to the feet of Jesus Christ where they will find life. Evangelism will be expressed in as many ways as there are people to express it.

We were created to know and enjoy God forever. Out of this intended purpose we will experience freedom and all that goes with it. It becomes a life rich in meaning and value. I have seen too much emphasis being placed on pursuing the meaningfulness and usefulness. This pursuit becomes fruitless when it is separated from our primary objective — to know and enjoy God forever. The meaning and purpose we long for is an outcome of a personal and intimate relationship with our creator.

Rest:

The life of service will require rest. A supernatural life will not be easy or effortless. On the contrary it will often be difficult and taxing. The difference between working hard and serving is seen in the hearts of people, not in the ease of the task. It requires a great deal of wisdom and discernment to know how to balance and pace your life. Guard your primary pursuit — knowing and enjoying God. Listen for the voice of God to speak to you and motivate you, not the voice of man. Do not imagine yourself so important that a job cannot get done without you. Know when to say, "No." Know when to make rest a priority. If God saw the value in resting, then we must value rest also. Jesus would separate Himself from everyone in order to receive needed rest and solitude with His father. We must look to His example.

Remember that a life of service is an outcome of the relationship you have with Christ. If we allow the outcome of our relationship with Jesus (service) to become our primary pursuit, then we have lost sight of our created purpose, to know and enjoy God forever. I have watched as God has led me into this, out of that, and then back into this other thing over here. There is a season for all things. A season spent in great exertion, and a season of slow paced rest. Don't fight either as being right or wrong. Accept God's direction and reap the blessing that both have to offer.

A life of service is both exciting and peaceful; it can be invigorating or calming. It is full of the pain that comes in loving others as Jesus loves others. With eyes and ears to see and understand the condition of mankind, we will suffer along with Christ. We will suffer for ourselves and for others. We will be lonely, and alone. We will belong and enjoy close fellowship. This life of service will be absolutely full of every experience that Jesus Himself experienced. Our every experience, as it is experienced in fellowship with God, will become a meaningful, useful part of our life of service.

Study Questions

Chapter Seventeen
Free to Serve

Freedom to serve! It hardly seems possible that freedom could look like service. The world would equate freedom with ____________ ____

Service is supernatural and can only come from a supernatural love. We can love the one who expects us to __________________, without feeling compelled to ___________________.

We learn that the transformed life is not about performance; it is about loving others well. It is about a love that offers grace and truth. It offers a grace that draws sinners toward us and not away. It offers a kind of truth that convicts, but does not condemn.
Psalm 51:13 teaches us about one of the beautiful outcomes of the transformed life: "Then I will teach transgressors thy ways, and sinners shall be converted unto thee."

We were created for "Good works."
"For by grace you have been saved through faith; and this is not your own doing, it is the gift of God – not because of works, lest any man should boast. For we are his workmanship, created in Christ Jesus for good works, which God prepared beforehand, that we should walk in them" (Ephesians 2:8-10).

The Spirit of God sets us free to give up a life of _______________ ___ and enter into a life of ________________ ________________.
In going from "works" to "good works" we find that the task we commit ourselves to may not change at all, because it is not about the task. "Good works" are not about what we ___________, it is about how we ________________. Sometimes loving others will be about "doing" things. (Physical acts of service) Sometimes loving others will consist of being there for someone emotionally. (Talking

through difficult issues with a friend, or being available in a time of need.)

My mother draws people to her kitchen counter like bees to honey. It is not because of the open door/open fridge policy that has always been the rule in her family home. It is because of the unconditional love and acceptance that people find when they spend time visiting with her over a glass of cold lemonade or a cup of hot tea. She does not shy away from any topic, however difficult it might be. She will tell you how wonderful you are and rejoice over all your minor victories in life. She will also call sin a sin and you won't feel any less loved for her having spoken the truth. My five siblings and I have always had a place to return to when we have created messes in our lives. (And we have accumulatively created more than our share of messes.) My mother and father successfully created a home that draws people to their kitchen counter. It is not about what they do, it is about how they love.

Think of a time when someone demonstrated love toward you through a physical act of service. ______________________________

____

Think of a time when someone demonstrated love toward you by providing support or advice. ______________________________

____

If you found yourself in need of emotional support or advice, who would you choose to go to in order to get that need met?

____

Are there individuals in your social circle that you would be more apt to approach with matters of the heart, and some individuals you would be less likely to trust with those heart issues? ____________

____

____

What is it about those trusted people that draws you to them? What is it about the love they emanate that makes them feel safe enough in order for you to be vulnerable? ______________________________

____

____

Ultimately, it is how we love others that will draw them, not only to us, but also to the feet of Jesus.
You won't need to ________________ this thing called evangelism. It will be a supernatural outcome of God's grace being expressed through you. "Sinners shall be converted unto thee" (Psalm 51:13 KJV).

Prayer: Father, I want my love for others to be like honey to a bee. I ask You, please, to love others through me with a love that draws sinners toward me and not away – with a love that convicts but does not condemn. Thank You for the people You have put in my life that love me well. Thank You that Your love for me is the only completely unshakable love that anchors my life.

Chapter Eighteen

Freedom

Here we have come to the final chapter in our study of the transformed life. Permit me to speak from my heart one final time, as I recap the key points that I hope we will all take with us.

The freedom we are seeking cannot happen in our lives until the Spirit of God is first able to reveal the truth to us about our sinful condition. At the risk of sounding utterly redundant, I must stress again that we will only experience the grace of God and love for God in proportion to how clearly we see our sin. Until we see clearly the ugliness of our self-centered hearts, we will not hate sin. It is in hating sin that we will finally be empowered to overcome it. That is when we begin to understand that there is not enough "willpower" in any of us to conquer the lure of sin. Only in hating sin will we have the strength to say "no" to sin.

When we experience God's response to our sinfulness (forgiveness), then our hearts become full of gratitude and awe at His unconditional love. God's grace towards us puts us in the position to be dispensers of grace toward others. Willpower is no longer what we look to as our strength — the joy of the Lord becomes our strength. God turns our sorrow to joy.

Those of you who have overcome addictions understand that of which I speak. Until you hated the addiction that gripped you, you were not fully able to overcome it. Willpower was certainly not the answer.

We were created to be dependent on God. It is the only dependency that will fill the longings of our hearts. We will either be slaves to Christ or slaves to sin. There is a price to pay when we are slaves to sin. We have all paid that price in our hearts: The absence of peace, lack of hope, and the inability to love responsibly are what we are left with in our sinful state. When we turn our dependency to Christ we experience life with meaning, and love without condition. We experience a peace that passes all understanding; peace in spite of the conditions or circumstances we find ourselves in. We find ourselves loving others in the face of all our fears (i.e., failure, rejection, abandonment). We will find ourselves beginning to love responsibly and unconditionally those who put conditions on us.

When we hate sin, the fight of the flesh loosens its grip and we begin to experience victory in the fight of faith. Our faith in God gives us a desire to obey. Obedience opens the floodgates of God's blessings. Obedience will lead us to understanding more and more of God's truth. We will be transformed by the truth.

What is Important to Freedom?:

God's will for us is transformation, and transformation is proof that God's will is happening in our lives. Meekness and humility will always be part of the proof of a transformed life. Are you looking to external things as you seek God's will in your life? If you are, then you might be having a difficult time in finding God's will. The proof will happen within you, not outside of you. The proof of transformation will look like qualities that resemble Christ's. These qualities include… meekness, humility, love, joy, peace, patience, goodness, kindness, gentleness, faithfulness, and self-control. It is the fruit of the Spirit that God desires to see in our lives. The fruit is where the proof lies. Too often, we look for the *gifts of the Spirit* rather than the *fruit of the Spirit* when looking for the proof of transformation. Scripture teaches us that the gifts alone are nothing.

~~~~~~~~~~~~~~~~~~~~

"If I speak in the tongues of men and of angels,
but have not love, I am a noisy gong or a clanging
~~~~~~~~~~~~~~~~~~~~

> cymbal. And if I have prophetic powers, and understand all mysteries and all knowledge, and if I have all faith, so as to remove mountains, but have not love, I am nothing. If I give away all I have and if I deliver my body to be burned, but have not love, I gain nothing" (I Corinthians 13:1-3).

~~~~~~~~~~~~~~~~~~~~

The gifts of the Spirit mentioned here (tongues, prophecy, wisdom, knowledge, faith, giving, and martyrdom) count as nothing if the fruit of the Spirit is not present. The fruit of love is God's primary concern. "Make love your aim…" (I Corinthians 14:1a). The gifts of the Spirit are a tremendous blessing, both to the community of believers and to each one of us individually. I am grateful that God allows us each to impact the world around us in ways we can enjoy as we respond to the personal motivation He gives us. Our primary goal, however, is to a higher calling. It is the calling to love your neighbor, yourself, and your enemy. God asks us to do good to those who hate us, bless those who curse us, and pray for those who abuse us. It is a challenge that renders us helpless. In our helplessness we may call on the Spirit of God to show us the way to love.

The fruit that comes from God living *in* us and *through* us is proof that God's will is happening in our lives. This is the life that He offers us. This is the freedom we experience in Christ. We are not called to perform in certain ways, or do certain things in the power of our flesh. In the flesh the Christian life is nothing more than an invitation to work hard and perform to the best of our ability. Our flesh, or natural selves, will not have God's supernatural resources from which to draw. God's Holy Spirit becomes our source of supernatural strength as we invite Him to love through us. God does not call us to be burnt out, tired, and weary. He calls us to be with Him. As a result, He will equip us to go out with the power to serve. Where we serve will not be God's primary concern. We can serve anywhere, anytime. The question is, are we able to serve? Have we been transformed from a life of "works," to a life of "service"? Do we understand that serving is about relating to others in truth with
~~~~~~~~~~~~~~~~~~~~

eyes and ears that are able to respond to the heart of the one we may be privileged to serve.

This life of service cannot be maintained without our being prepared to do battle against the lies that the enemy would have us believe. By taking every thought captive and holding it up to what we know to be true, we can, and will be transformed one thought at a time. We will experience the power of truth as it not only sets us free but also keeps us free.

<u>What is Not Important to Freedom?:</u>

To thirst for truth is to thirst for God.

~~~~~~~~~~~~~~~~~~~~

"As a deer longs for flowing streams, so my soul longs for you, O God" (Psalm 42:1 NRSV).

~~~~~~~~~~~~~~~~~~~~

To know Jesus is to know the truth. Jesus says, "I am ... the truth" (John 14:6). The more we experience Jesus in truth, the better we become at handling every captive thought. Therefore, get to know Him. That is my message to you. It is the only encouragement I care to give you. There is no other concern I have for you. The traditions and trappings that entangle the body of Christ are of little concern to me. I care not whether you were sprinkled as a baby or dunked as an adult. I am not interested in whether or not you believe in a pre-trib, mid-trib, or post-trib rapture. I care little about what your spiritual gifts are. Whether you teach, or preach, or speak in the tongues of angels, I care not. If you do not have a current, living, fruitful life in Christ you are nothing but a clanging cymbal. I do not care which denominational name you attach to yourself. I do care about one thing. It is what Jesus cared about with the people that were close to Him. It is the first question; it is the only question. Jesus, Himself, asks this question of you... "Who do you say that I am?"

The answer to that question and how you respond to it either unites us and puts us on common ground, or it separates us for eternity. If we agree that Jesus is who He says He is, and we call on Him in order to accept the offering of His life, and in turn give to Him our life, then we agree on the only thing that need be agreed on.

Please do not speak disparagingly of my brothers and sisters who represent denominations other than your own. They are my friends. Do not waste words trying to convince a brother or sister to believe as you do on a minor issue that will in no way encourage them to know Jesus or become more intimate with Him. The only thing worth putting our energy into is our personal relationship to the one we call Christ.

The encouragement we need is to walk with Him, and talk with Him always. In knowing Him you will know the truth. The truth will set you free — free to love Him. Your love for Him will enable you to obey. Being free to obey, you will grow eyes to see. Freedom to see and understand the truth will transform your mind. Your new mind will set you free to serve. The servant life that Jesus demonstrated for us while He walked this earth is what a life of freedom looks like. It is the abundant life that He desires for each one of us. It is not about doing what Jesus did. It is about being free to love as Jesus loved. During His short stay on earth He modeled a love that came out of a simple and total dependence on His Father in heaven. Without the Father, He could do nothing. Neither can we. We must simply depend on Him with every breath we take, and allow Him to live in us, and through us. Watch and see what the Christian life looks like as you give your life over to Him.

Living With Jesus:

1. Practice Gods presence. Turn to Him constantly throughout the day and talk to Him. Make Him your best friend. After you have talked to Him, listen to Him in silence. Experience the new thoughts that will flood your mind. Experience God speaking to you.

Talk to Him often, and about everything. Corrie Ten Boom says, "Satan often laughs when we work, but he shudders when we pray." If prayer can do that, then we have indeed begun to fight the right fight in the right way — the fight of faith.

2. Spend time in the Bible. Every time you open God's word, ask God to guide you and teach you. You must invite Him to do this.

With the Holy Spirit as your teacher, it will begin to fill you with the knowledge and the fullness of your God. When you invite Him to teach you, you can be certain He will do it, for it is His will that it be done. The Bible, for us as Christians, is living and active when the Spirit of God reveals to us the mysteries that lie within it. The Spirit of God reveals truth to us that we could not otherwise comprehend. Only the Holy Spirit can reveal truth to us in a way that we will see and understand.

> "For what person knows a man's thoughts except the spirit of the man which is in him? So also no one comprehends the thoughts of God except the Spirit of God. Now we have received not the spirit of the world, but the Spirit which is from God, that we might understand the gifts bestowed on us by God. And we impart this in words not taught by human wisdom but taught by the Spirit, interpreting spiritual truths to those who possess the Spirit" (I Corinthians 2:11-13).

The truth as the Holy Spirit reveals it to you will set you free. If this were not true, the Pharisees would have indeed been free. They knew the Bible backwards and forwards, but it had no power in their lives. It was a book full of rules — it was lifeless — it was law. Many of us today read Scripture in the same way the Pharisees did long ago. George MacDonald writes, "Wise and prudent religious men interpret the great heart of God, not by their own hearts, but by their intellects. Then, postponing the obedience that alone can give power to the understanding, they press upon men's minds their low interpretations of the will of the Father, instead of by their own example impressing the doing of that will upon their hearts. They are the slaves of the letter in all its weakness and imperfection — and will be until the Spirit of the Word, the Spirit of obedience, shall set them free."[16]

Invite the Spirit of God to do what He so desires to do; teach you the truth by which you will be set free.

~~~~~~~~~~~~~~~~~~~~

> "Such is the confidence that we have through Christ toward God. Not that we are competent of ourselves to claim anything as coming from us; our competence is from God, who has made us competent to be ministers of a new covenant, not in a written code but in the spirit; for the written code kills, but the spirit gives life" (II Corinthians 3:4-6).
>
> "Now the Lord is the Spirit, and where the spirit of the Lord is, there is freedom. And we all, with unveiled face, beholding the glory of the Lord, are being changed into his likeness from one degree of glory to another; for this comes from the Lord who is the spirit!" (II Corinthians 3:17-18)

~~~~~~~~~~~~~~~~~~~~

Spend time in the word being taught by the spirit of God!!

These two things will keep you focused. They will keep your mind clear, so that you will recognize the truth when you hear it, and you will recognize a lie when you hear it. Keep your focus always on Jesus. When we lose sight of Him, we lose perspective. We must learn to turn to Him continually and recognize his presence. You cannot grow enough spiritually so that you are no longer susceptible to losing sight of Him. You cannot grow enough spiritually so that you can coast for a while. Your time with God cannot be stored up and tapped into at a future date. Just like the manna in the wilderness, they could only store up enough for one day or it would rot. So it is in your life with Christ. You must pray this day for your daily bread. You must turn this day to your Lord and Savior. You need to recognize His presence at all times and in all situations. Don't ever let intimacy with God become a memory. Keep it a reality. Don't live your life based on a past relationship you once had with Jesus. Live your life based on the relationship you have with Him today.

As we begin to know our Lord; as we grow more and more intimate with God; then we will begin to believe in God's love with a faith that believes without seeing. We will experience the transforming power of the Holy Spirit as we daily invite him to live not only in us, but also through us. We will begin to recognize the truth when we hear it, and we will be able to discern a lie when we hear it. We will begin to know the life on earth that He intends for us to live. It is a life of freedom in Christ. The curtain is torn! It is possible!

Study Questions

Chapter Eighteen
Freedom

When looking for the proof of transformation in our lives, we often look for the gifts of the Spirit. While the spiritual gifts are a tremendous blessing to all of us, it is the fruit of the Spirit that God is wanting to see grow in us.

~~~~~~~~~~~~~~~~~~~~

> "If I speak in the tongues of men and of angels, but have not love, I am a noisy gong or a clanging cymbal. And if I have prophetic powers, and understand all mysteries and all knowledge, and if I have all faith, so as to remove mountains, but have not love, I am nothing. If I give away all I have and if I deliver my body to be burned, but have not love, I gain nothing: (I Corinthians 13:1-3).

~~~~~~~~~~~~~~~~~~~~

God's love, as it is expressed through you, will set you free to live the servant life. It is a life rich with blessing.

As Christians we often lose sight of our primary aim. I Corinthians 14:1 tells us to make ________________ our primary aim.

It is easy for our focus to shift to traditions that can entangle the body of Christ. What are some areas that you have seen put a rift in the body of Christ? ______________________________________

____

____

What is the most important part of your faith to you personally, and to those with whom you desire to share your faith? ______________

____

____

In living with Jesus, what two things does chapter eighteen encourage you to make part of your daily life?

1) ____

____

____

2) ____

____

____

Reflecting back on the book, is there anything that God spoke to you personally about that you hope to remember? If so, what is it He taught you? ____

____

____

____

God wants us to remember the things He teaches us. He provides a way for us to remember...

~~~~~~~~~~~~~~~~~~~~

> "But the Counselor, the Holy Spirit, whom the Father will send in my name, he will teach you all things and bring to your remembrance all that I have said to you. Peace I leave with you; my peace I give to you; not as the world gives do I give to you. Let not your hearts be troubled, neither let them be afraid... Rise, let us go hence" (John 14:26-27,31b).

~~~~~~~~~~~~~~~~~~~~

~~~~~~~~~~~~~~~~~~~~

"For I know the plans I have for you," declares the Lord, "plans to prosper you and not to harm you, plans to give you hope and a future. Then you will call upon me and come and pray to me, and I will listen to you. You will seek me and find me when you seek me with all your heart. I will be found by you," declares the Lord, "and will bring you back from captivity" (Jeremiah 29:11-14a NIV).

~~~~~~~~~~~~~~~~~~~~

The Curtain Is Torn

Knowing Jesus
personally and intimately.

In knowing Jesus,
you will know the truth.
Jesus is the truth.

The truth will set you
Free.

Free to obey.

Free to see.

Free to love.

Free to serve.

Transformation!

Endnotes

1. Jeff VanVonderen, *Tired of Trying to Measure Up* (Bethany House Publishers, 1989), p. 41

2. Jill Briscoe, Address, Hope Presbyterian Church, Richfield, MN, Circa 1990.

3. James Packard, Address, Huron Hills Baptist Church, Ann Arbor, MI, June 1987.

4. VanVonderen, p. 20.

5. VanVonderen, p. 101.

6. Jeffrey Satinover, M.D., *Homosexuality and the Politics of Truth*, (Hamewith Books, 1997) p.146.

7. Dr. Henry Cloud and Dr. John Townsend, *Boundaries,* (Zondervan Publishing House, 1992), p.30.

8. George MacDonald, *Discovering the Character of God,* (Bethany House Publishers, 1989), p. 44.

9. John M. Gottman, Ph.D., *The Seven Principles For Making Marriage* Work (Three Rivers Press, 1999), p. 27.

10. Gottman, *p.29.*

11. A.W. Tozer, *Keys to the Deeper Life* (Bethany House Publishers, 1989), p.66.

12. Nancy Groom, *From Bondage to Bonding*, (NavPress, 1991), p.26-27.

13. Groom, p. 47.

14. Dr. John Townsend, *Hiding From Love,* Zondervan Publishing House, 82.

15. Groom, p. 27.

16. MacDonald, p. 136.

Printed in the United States
58599LVS00006B/7-144

9 781600 341281